THE COACHING SECRET

How to be an exceptional coach

ANDREW MACHON

Prentice Hall Business is an imprint of

 PEARSON

D0321340

Marlow, England • London • New York • Boston • San Francisco • Toronto • Sydney • Singapore • Hong Kong
Tokyo • Seoul • Taipei • New Delhi • Cape Town • Madrid • Mexico City • Amsterdam • Munich • Paris • Milan

PEARSON EDUCATION LIMITED

Edinburgh Gate
Harlow CM20 2JE
Tel: +44 (0)1279 623623
Fax: +44 (0)1279 431059
Website: www.pearsoned.co.uk

First published in Great Britain in 2010

ISBN: 978-0-273-72460-5

British Library Cataloguing-in-Publication Data
A catalogue record for this book is available from the British Library

Library of Congress Cataloging-in-Publication Data
Machon, Andrew.
  The coaching secret / Andrew Machon.
      p. cm.
  ISBN 978-0-273-72460-5 (pbk.)
  1.   Personal coaching. 2.   Executive coaching.   I. Title.
  BF637 .P36M33 2009
  158' .3--dc22

                                                                  2009039560

10 9 8 7 6 5 4 3 2 1
13 12 11 10 09

Typeset in 12/16pt Ehrhardt MT by 35
Printed by Ashford Colour Press Ltd, Gosport

The publisher's policy is to use paper manufactured from sustainable forests.

To my Father, who encouraged me to write and shared in the excitement of the journey

CONTENTS

•••

ACKNOWLEDGEMENTS

• • •

Primarily, I wish to acknowledge the continuous support and guidance of Dr Gwil Roberts. His dependability and unwavering enthusiasm, affection and collaborative intelligence have carried me forward each step of the way, particularly in moments of uncertainty and self-doubt.

Those who play a vital role in facilitating development often go unseen. Not unlike the coach, the role of the commissioning editor can at times seem to be that of an unsung hero, or heroine in my case. Without the guidance, expert knowledge, sensitivity and creative insight of Samantha Jackson, my commissioning editor at Pearson Education, quite simply, this book would not have been written. Samantha's unique contribution is to bring out the very best. The greatest gift has been meeting an inspiring editor who, at the time of completing this book, has become a treasured friend.

My gratitude goes to Dr Piers Worth, a truly masterful practitioner whose quality of attention and guidance I have greatly appreciated.

My thanks also go to my twin brother, Adrian Machon, for his insightful conversations and guidance in concluding this work, and a ring of coaches who have inspired the birth of this book, including Dr Tom Sappington, Val Tomlin, Dr Ed Young, Dr Julie Schofield, Trish Baron, Helen Chapman and Alison Griffiths.

Central to this book is the knowledge and learning that has arisen through my coaching and supervisory relationships. I feel greatly privileged to have been a witness and guide. My heartfelt gratitude goes to each and all.

INTRODUCTION

...

This book will be a valuable guide to all those who coach, irrespective of your level of experience. Coaching centres on the occupation of the coach, yet from my knowledge the ability to coach is increasingly employed in many other professions, including leadership, management, mentoring, counselling, parenting and teaching. The coaching relationship may be the key vehicle through which the individual, group and organisation are able to make and sustain change.

For those newly entering this occupation this book will provide an insight into how you can build your confidence and expertise to coach. It explores how you may answer some of the essential questions you are likely to be asked. It will help you to understand more deeply and appreciate the work and journey of the coach and encourage your apprenticeship. To the experienced practitioner this work examines the scope of coaching, how the field is evolving and maturing and the secret of how to be or become an exceptional coach. Through examples taken from my own practice we will explore together how to discover the vision, essential instruments, identity, role, qualities and faculties of the masterful coach.

It is interesting to find that much of our coaching literature presents only a partial view of coaching. This is an exterior view that looks at coaching from the 'outside in' and places emphasis on the facts. This same view is favoured and selected by the leaders and managers who are often the key employers of the business coach. What is brought into focus from this viewpoint is the definition, methodology, process and the external tools of coaching – the 'what' of coaching. This view creates a picture of coaching as an occupation that places an emphasis on measurably improving performance and business success. Organisations and coaches alike may often quite unwittingly conspire in believing that this is all there is to coaching – helping to create an exclusive self-fulfilling prophecy.

While recognising the value and place of this perspective as one important piece of our repertoire, twenty years of coaching experience suggests that there is something missing. My quest as a coach has always been to understand the nature of how we develop, learn and grow – that is, how the coach can help the clients to make the sustained changes they desire.

That word *sustained* is key here, and although an exterior view of coaching can have an impact on skills development and even behavioural change, increasingly I believe we may need to include an interior view of coaching to help clients to learn how to shift beliefs, identity and sense of self to make the sustained changes they desire. Only with a combined exterior and interior vision can we help our clients to realise their hidden potential and make these sustained changes, while fostering integrity and a more authentic approach to work. Whereas the 'what' of coaching is of value, to discover the truly masterful coach the additional questions we really need to ask ourselves are the 'why', 'how' and 'who' of coaching.

Many thousands of new coaches continue to enter the field each year. As significant numbers have a very limited training, and have little experience of coaching or supervision, I am sometimes concerned that coaching may be wrongly perceived as an easy option. While understanding how this mistake can happen, you will commonly hear or read, particularly in coach-training literature, that no expert knowledge is required to become a coach.

Think about this point of view carefully. If you are coaching business executives, for example, you do not require their technical expertise. However, to coach well does require an expertise – a personal expertise. Do not be mistaken, coaching is not a superficial practice or an easy option. The capacity to focus purely on the activity of coaching without distraction, and giving your full concentration and attentiveness to the client, is a rare and cultivated talent. From my experience this talent is learned from the inside out and necessitates an inner journey. Watching a masterful coach in action, you will often see a lightness of touch and sense of freedom. These do not come from naïveté and inexperience, they are born from a deep self-awareness and acceptance, as we will explore.

Self-awareness and acceptance are what I call 'relative knowledge' – your ability to coach emerges from a commitment to your own personal journey and inner learning: *you* ultimately become your own tutor and guide. Through coaching you remember and discover the identity of your inner coach, whose natural talent and mastery inform your practice. As we learn to manage ourselves, the coach within becomes free to help guide others to the threshold of their learning.

Some years ago I was asked to talk to a group of leaders and managers about the value and nature of coaching. Even then I was curious about the reflective vision of the coach and how this could be best understood and shared. While musing about an image that might help to explain this, the Roman God Janus entered my mind. Janus has two heads that look in opposite directions and has thus the unique ability to see in two different directions simultaneously. This image of Janus fits well with the requirements of being and becoming a masterful coach.

To coach well, you need to be able both to observe and reflect – to see objectively and to sense subjectively. I often imagine the coach as a living mirror which, when operated with mastery, becomes a two-way 'Janus like' mirror. The mirror is an essential instrument of the coach and we will see how this combines with the lens and compass to form the inner toolkit of the masterful coach.

The masterful coach has an evolved vision and ability to sense that includes different ways of seeing – different 'eyes'. I call these the analytical eye, the appreciative eye and the creative eye. Each has contrasting viewpoints – different visions of reality that impact upon and inform the way you coach in practice.

When you look from the 'outside in', you employ an analytical eye that offers the coach a one-dimensional (1D) viewpoint that is partial, objective and detached. When you look from the 'inside out', you open an appreciative eye that has a two-dimensional (2D) vision that is both subjective and relational. The vision of the appreciative eye extends beyond our rational awareness. By accommodating both the analytical and appreciative eyes together, the coach opens the creative eye. This offers you a dynamic 3D vision that is more unlimited and can span the objective–subjective divide – *the* essential component of mastery. This eye allows you to expand your awareness of the collective and universal as well as of the individual.

In your journey towards mastery, your work as a coach will change from one of tutor and instructor, to one who becomes a compassionate co-creator of your own and your client's highest future potential and possibility. It is easy to misjudge and wrongly devalue the work of the coach as superficial. Coaching is an enigmatic profession that is learned largely on the job. It is also hard, if not impossible, to rationalise how the work of the coach can have such a positive impact on the learning of the client. But it is important not to reject the enigmatic dimension of the coaching work – if you do, you will never truly discover the secret behind masterful coaching.

I believe there is a masterful coach in each and all of us that we are invited to discover. The secret of being an exceptional coach is in realising that mastery is lost the moment we seek it as something other than our most natural and innate talent and motivation to change. In becoming masterful, we discover the source of our potential and can plumb the depth of our humanity and authenticity, while discovering how to see, sense, relate and resolve.

I do not see my way of coaching as the right way or suggest that I am a master coach. To do so goes against the nature of the very principle and secret of mastery:

Mastery is a gift we permit ourselves when we tire of the need to be right or better

My goal in this book is simply to share my experience of being a coach in an open-hearted way that I hope may inspire debate and enhance practice, with the intent to expand awareness of our occupation and the wider field of coaching.

In reading this book you will take the journey of being and becoming a masterful coach. Each chapter concerns a response to an essential question of coaching and in its entirety will help you to answer each of the following questions:

- What is coaching?
- Why do we coach?
- How does the vision and essential instrumentation of the coach develop?
- How does super-vision support and encourage the development of the coach?
- Who is – and what is the role of – a masterful coach?
- How do we experience masterful practice and what are the distinctive faculties and qualities of the masterful coach?

Most importantly, we will see how the key to becoming an exceptional, masterful coach is already in your hands.

Chapter One

WHAT IS COACHING?

• • •

In this chapter, we will study the basic coaching process and the characteristics of the coaching conversation, distilling the key aspects of the work of the coach. Exploring a historical perspective of coaching will help us to realise how the response to 'What is coaching?' provides only a partial and incomplete picture. This brings us to the conclusion that a comprehensive definition of coaching remains elusive.

• • •

The answer to 'What is coaching?' is neither simple nor straightforward. We think that it ought to be, and is, possible to provide a single comprehensive definition of coaching. After many years of coaching, I am still unable to solve this conundrum. The responses to the question of 'What is coaching?'

give us a whole constellation of different facts and facets. But these only provide a partial picture and, no matter how hard we try to define this view, we may never reach a single answer. Let us examine responses to 'What is coaching?' and collect together some of the key pieces of this puzzle.

• THE FOUR ESSENTIAL ELEMENTS OF THE COACHING PROCESS •

Literature on coaching presents a number of iterations and permutations of the basic process. My goal here is to crystallise the essential elements of the coaching process, and provide a basic platform on which we can build.

PAUSE POINT

Take a moment to jot down how you see the basic coaching process. See if you can select what the key elements are from your own understanding and experience of coaching.

The coach basically helps to guide the client to do four key things in an iterative way:

1 To be more open and aware.
2 To clarify a desired goal.
3 To expand awareness around this goal.
4 To focus, respond and realise the desired outcome.

If you think of this iterative process in three dimensions it takes the form of an increasing spiral of improved performance, development and learning, as illustrated in Figure 1 (opposite).

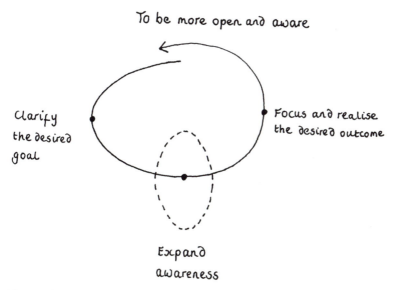

To be more open and aware

Clarify
the desired
goal

Focus and realise
the desired outcome

Expand
awareness

Figure 1

THE COACHING FRAME – HELPING THE CLIENT TO BE OPEN AND AWARE

The essential elements of coaching happen within a window of time, where the client steps out of their routine into the coaching frame and goes back again. This frame marks out a time and a place that are set aside for coaching. Your purpose in setting the coaching frame is to create an environment where the clients feel very safe and comfortable – a place where they are willing to face and will contract to deal with their real challenges. This frame is a kind of safe container and somewhere the clients can find a trusting relationship, feel heard and are open to challenge and exploration. The importance of the coaching frame and its key aspects are illustrated in Figure 2 (p.10).

Within this frame you may explain a little about what coaching is, answer any pressing questions, share what you ideally would

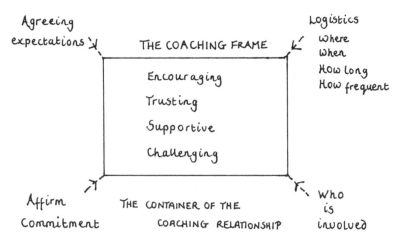

Figure 2

like to happen and something of your experience of coaching to help the client to build trust and confidence. It presents the ideal chance for you to affirm your commitment to the client's development and growth and to explore how this can be encouraged.

You'll also need to agree the logistics and the practicalities of meeting and of working together; the time, duration and frequency of each session as well as the total period over which the coaching will initially extend. And you can agree if other individuals will be involved – examples may include the sponsor of the coaching work or peers who are keen to provide the client with feedback relevant to the coaching.

The coaching frame is essentially a 'window' through which the clients can explore. Here they look outwardly into their environment or organisation, and look inwardly to explore what may be affecting their development, learning and performance.

CLARIFYING THE DESIRED GOAL

With the supportive frame in place, the activity of coaching can begin. A key step is to allow your client to explore the scope of their field of interest. This offers the coach a chance to get to know the client better through careful observation, listening and checking. It is valuable to gain an insight of your client's values and vision. The next key step is for the coach to help the client to clarify their goal by mirroring back key aspects of the conversation, checking perceptions and agreeing a shared understanding of the situation – coaching is a results- and solution-focused activity.

EXPANDING AWARENESS AROUND THE DESIRED GOAL

The third essential phase of coaching is where the coach guides the client to open and expand their awareness around a desired goal. Careful questioning, observation and the use of what I call the 'living mirror' of the coach largely achieve this. I cannot overemphasise the importance and value of this mirror to coaching. The living mirror is unique in its capacity to observe and reflect. Through this interaction, the client remembers and recognises their core attributes. It is through the living mirror as one of the essential instruments of the coach that the client is defined, constructed and co-created. The value of the mirror to the coach will be explored in more detail in Chapter 4.

FOCUS, RESPOND AND REALISE THE DESIRED OUTCOME

At the core of coaching is an ability to help to expand the client's awareness and focus their attention and learning. This dynamic expansion and contraction is at the heart of coaching. It allows the client to recognise new or different choices and to take firm steps towards their desired outcome. The coach helps the client to discover choices and is a witness to their commitment, encouraging the client's willingness to take responsibility and act to realise their desired goal.

COACHING FRAME

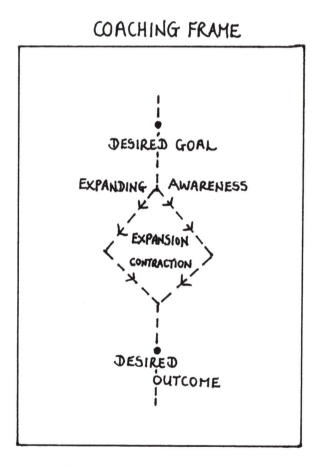

THE BASIC COACHING PROCESS

Figure 3

• THE BASIC PLATFORM •

If we think of the basic process of coaching as a platform on which we can build, then this is illustrated diagrammatically in Figure 3 (opposite), which shows the key dimensions we have discussed.

HOW IS THE CONVERSATION OF COACHING DIFFERENT TO ANY OTHER?

To demonstrate the difference that the basic elements of coaching make to conversation, let us compare everyday conversation with a coaching conversation.

A TYPICAL EVERYDAY CONVERSATION ABOUT WORK

Person 1:   How are things?

Person 2:   Not good. I'm not feeling good at all.

Person 1:   I'm not feeling too good either today.

Person 2:   I'm having problems with the boss.

Person 1:   I wouldn't put up with that if I were you.

Person 2:   I'm not sure what to do.

Person 1:   If you're unhappy you should get out – it's not worth it.

Person 2:   I *am* unhappy.

Person 1:   I've got a friend in a very similar position – she got out because she decided that no one was going to tell her what to do.

Person 2:   How's your work?

Person 1:   Couldn't be better.

Person 2:   I think I must be doing something wrong.

Person 1:   Maybe you are.

Person 2:   I worry about it.

Person 1:   My work's going great, things are going really well.

Person 2:   Lucky for some.

Person 1:	Hope to get promotion this year.
Person 2:	Promotions are rare in this organisation now.
Person 1:	Mine's due.
Person 2:	I think you'll be lucky – things are changing.
Person 1:	I think you're wrong on this one.
Person 2:	We'll see.
Person 1:	I don't want to rub it in but it's a cert.
Person 2:	I think you're mistaken.

A COACHING CONVERSATION

Coach:	What's important to you today?
Client:	Er (*pause*)... in truth (*pause*)... I'm concerned about my relationship with my new boss.
Coach:	You look very concerned. Tell me more?
Client:	We've not got off to a good start for some reason. I've a lot of experience in this job and I feel as though I'm being over-scrutinised.
Coach:	Mmm (*pause*). Tell me how does that impact you?
Client:	I feel as though I'm being watched. I feel boxed in, as if my freedom has been taken away.
Coach:	I see. Is there anything more?
Client:	(*Pause*) I don't know what I'm doing wrong.
Coach:	You may not be doing anything wrong (*pause*). How aware is your boss of how you feel?
Client:	Not at all, I'm wondering if it might be the time to sit down and explore with her why this is happening.
Coach:	What's your hunch why this is happening?
Client:	My boss is new to the role (*pause*). I don't think she's found her feet yet.
Coach:	How is it not to find your feet?

Client:	(*Pause*) Its scary I suppose.
Coach:	Scary?
Client:	Yes. When you're scared you tend to cling on and over-scrutinise (*pause*). Ah ha! Is that why I'm feeling micro-managed?
Coach:	Might your boss need something from you?
Client:	I might ask her (*pause*). Yes, I could ask her how it's going. Then explore if I can help in any way – with my experience. I would be happy to try that.
Coach:	Sounds like a part of an important conversation.
Client:	Yes

COMPARING CONVERSATIONS

What key generalisations can we draw, by comparing these conversations, that helps to develop our understanding about what coaching is? When the coaching frame has been agreed and the coach guides the process, the client is given full attention and questioned openly, the pace is slower and there is space to pause and reflect. In contrast, in the example of everyday conversation, little attention is given to either person and the questions asked are largely closed. The intention is commonly to prove your own point and rightness. In contrast, the focus of the coaching conversation is the client's exploration and learning.

• WHAT THE COACH DOES •

The coach guides and helps the client to develop and learn. Their approach is largely non-directive, though at times the coach may challenge or intervene to reframe situations. The answer to how the client can learn, and desires to learn, rests with the client, not with the coach. Once more the role of the coach is to help to guide the client to realise their inherent learning needs and fulfil them. While the coach employs their experience, the client is empowered to discover their own resourcefulness and conceive their own solution.

Very rarely does the coach instruct or direct: predominantly the role is one of guiding and facilitating

IS THE DICTIONARY DEFINITION OF COACHING OUT OF DATE?

If you were to turn to a dictionary or encyclopaedia to find out how coaching is defined, you may return doubly confused. The *Oxford Dictionary* defines the verb to coach as 'to tutor, train, give hints to and prime with facts'. The on-line encyclopaedia *Wikipedia* similarly describes coaching as 'a method of directing, instructing and training a person or a group of people, with the aim to achieve some goal or develop a specific skill'.

Both state that the central objective of coaching is tuition and instruction. This description and definition of coaching bears little resemblance to the actual role employed by the majority of the coaches of today. How can we make sense of this confusion? Can this confusion help us to answer and learn something more about what coaching is?

• COACHING IN CONTEXT •

In the early 1960s this was indeed an accurate definition of what coaching was thought to be, and sports coaches of this period worked by instruction, seeking to pass on their expert knowledge and experience to their clients. At this time the coach was viewed as the technical expert who taught and instructed the clients to learn.

In the 1970s our understanding of coaching changed quite profoundly. This was thanks to the pioneering work of Tim Gallwey who began publishing a series of books about the art and practice of sports coaching from 1974 onwards, one of which is featured in the suggested reading at the end of this book. What this pioneering work highlighted was something that turned our definition of coaching on its head – that instruction and tuition by the coach was more likely to inhibit the learning of the client than foster it.

The capacity to learn and develop is influenced by the client's own interior state. A directive and instructional approach can often magnify a fear of failure that can inhibit the client's capacity to learn. How our clients judge and criticise themselves can strongly interfere with their capacity to learn. The implication here is that development and learning is more self-directed than instructed, and originates from the inside out.

What was realised is that the client alone holds the key to unlock their own developmental learning and potential, and this is achieved by a process of self-management and self-discovery. Commonly, as we will explore, the client is blind to the control exerted by their inner voices of judgement and criticism. It is the role of the coach then to help the client to move past these barriers – a coach who has experience of the inner process of development and learning, who can adopt a largely non-directive approach. Coaches today, in my experience, largely support a non-directive and facilitative approach, so the dictionary definition of coaching appears to be quite out of date.

COACHING IN THE LITERATURE

Beyond the dictionary definition of coaching, the literature contains many different definitions. These differ and overlap, but all have a place and value. Each definition contains a number of the important facets of coaching that are highlighted from asking the question 'What is coaching?' and yet it seems quite impossible to find a single comprehensive definition from this approach.

In coaching literature, for example, we find that some coaching definitions highlight the importance of improving performance. Others seem to look deeper and place a focus on either development and learning or change. Some highlight the coaching conversation, others the coaching process.

Figure 4 (below) illustrates the many different interpretations of coaching and shows just how problematic it is to seek a single comprehensive definition. I see these different definitions as the pieces of a puzzle that can never quite be completed.

Figure 4

THE ELUSIVE DEFINITION OF COACHING

The need to define coaching is further complicated by how we strive to differentiate it from related professions such as mentoring, counselling, psychotherapy, management, leadership and parenting. We believe that it ought to have its own unique remit and differentiated niche. It is pertinent to stop and pause and consider whether, rather than seeking to define coaching, might we learn something more by resisting this temptation?

THE EVOLUTION OF COACHING

This is because no matter how much effort we place on seeking a single comprehensive definition of coaching that answers the question 'What is coaching?', it ever remains just beyond our reach. Might the role of coaching be less fixed than we imagine and maybe more of a moving target? Does the shift from the role of instructor to facilitator mark one of a number of significant steps along a continuum of learning? Instead of trying to define what coaching is, would it be more helpful to consider whether the coach plays several roles? Might the role of the coach be a wayfarer whose journey is inwards, with the object of discovering the person's nature and depth of humanity, and then using this to help to guide the performance, development and learning of others? We will explore and develop this topic more fully in Chapter 7.

COACHING AS FACT AND MYSTERY

Because of the coach's inward journey, coaching has an enigmatic quality, which, by its very nature, is difficult to pin down. I think of coaching as a natural blend of both fact and mystery.

Our rational thinking treats mystery as if it were the vast unknown and will fear and reject its existence. But in our need for certainty let us not throw the baby out with the bath water. Might it be that an exploration of the coaching enigma gives us a deeper understanding of what coaching is and, in turn, may lead us to masterful practice?

If you can accept this invitation, then your need to define lessens. What emerges is the possibility of a more integrative vision of coaching. This vision can see and acknowledge how the basic coaching skills may be valuable to, and employed in, other occupations. Can we open our minds a little more to explore and accommodate a wider and deeper appreciation of what coaching might be? Only with this integrated vision are we able to see both the wider scope and focus of coaching and so support the possibility of its continuing emergence and evolution.

Mindful of this invitation, let's now consider why we coach and explore how this provides insight to the nature of coaching and masterful practice.

Chapter Two

WHY WE COACH

• • •

The response to 'Why do we coach?' leads to what is missing – the remembrance of the inner source and origin of your potential and power. Here we explore the existence of two iterations of self – both a partial and whole self. This potentiality towards becoming more whole is a measure of your desire to make sustained change and the motivation to become the person you aspire to be.

• • •

In seeking to answer the question 'What is coaching?' we have looked at this occupation from different angles. Each angle is like a piece of a puzzle but, no matter how hard we try, these different pieces do not connect together to complete a full picture. The 'what' offers only a partial view and reminds us that coaching is a composite of both fact and mystery. How can we more fully enter into the mystery of coaching to discover what we might be missing and what will help to complete our understanding? I believe that we can explore what is missing by responding to another question: 'Why do we coach?'

To explore this fundamental question, it is useful here for me to draw directly on my own experience and ask myself this very question.

On the surface, I wish to help others to develop within business and organisational settings, and to feel happier and more fulfilled in their working lives. Beneath this I am also tirelessly curious about human nature, who I am and how we develop, learn and grow. Coaching offers the chance to explore the generative nature of a trusting relationship and, in fact, how we learn to relate.

Part of my wish to become a coach reflects the need to know and understand myself much better. This learning equally harbours the wish to help others to better understand themselves and to grow. Deeper still, I realise that I am somehow drawn to coaching.

This is not an occupation I have chosen at random. Coaching is, in many ways, my most natural occupation. I feel somehow 'called' to coaching. What I mean is, while wanting outwardly to develop others, something inside equally longs to be developed. Does our motivation to coach reflect a deeper longing to grow ourselves?

• POWER AND POTENTIAL •

In answering the question 'Why do I coach?', I acknowledge the aspect that motivates my development and growth and affirm the existence of a source of new possibility and power to be found within. Is this the source of hidden potential that we each and all wish to harness and into which our organisations long to tap? Is this our hidden resource that appears to be the origin of our aspirations and longing, our passion and purpose, our performance and productivity, our deeper humanity and authenticity, our creative expression and well-being?

If we are able to stay with the 'why', then we can remember the origin of our desire to coach and have access to its hidden potential and power. If we are unable to reflect and question, then we overlook this source and become increasingly blind to its possibility. To become masterful we must discover the vital importance of being inwardly directed and how we can learn to see or sense potentiality.

THE COACHING BLIND SPOT

If we recall our response to the 'what' of coaching you will now see how this focuses on the surface facts and overlooks the depth and true source of our power and potential. The 'what' is concerned with the facts, process and methods of the coach and how our performance may be quantitatively measured, and yet it overlooks the true source of our desire and motivation to change and develop.

> Without knowledge and a working insight to the existence of our deeper authenticity and humanity, the coach and client are blind to the source of power that motivates all sustained change.

It is not the work of the coach to predict or know what the client needs or aspires to achieve, this content is purely personal to the client. What is required of the coach is an awareness of their original source of learning and power so that they can help to guide the client to realise this possibility.

• TWO SELVES •

The 'why' of coaching puts us back in touch with the person we often overlook. This is the person we aspire to be or become. How can we best describe this self? It is your most natural and genuine self; who you are when you are content, happy and growing. Becoming this person offers the chance for you to realise your fuller potential and to feel more real, natural and fulfilled. In realising this deeper self we can express the source of our motivation to learn and develop.

In exploring both the 'what' and the 'why' of coaching we therefore recognise the existence of two different but related selves. The first is your everyday self. It is the self that you present outwardly to the world – your outer face. When you forget to question and ask 'why', this concept of self seems to be fixed and to mark the full extent of your identity. However, when you reflect and recognise the person you wish to become, you realise that there is conceivably another iteration of self that you recall and can potentially become. We are drawn to this second self – a 'self in potential' – as it represents the person we would ideally like to be and desire to become. Is this our most natural original self? The vision of the masterful coach is sensitive to and guided by this potentiality, seeing that, beneath the need to improve performance, is the wish of the client to realise their second, most natural, self.

This second self motivates your development. It is the self that you were born to be.

Against the second self, the first self appears partial. Awareness of the second self means that the first can no longer be the full extent of identity – it is a deeper sense of identity and source, it is, once more, the person you aspire to be.

COACHING AND THE TWO SELVES

Why are two selves important to coaching? As we have established, the existence of the second self implies that the self we commonly present to the world is partial. The recognition of both selves offers a direction and meaning to our development – that we are not fixed, but, rather, in the process of becoming. The desired goal of the client is also to 'become' – to become the person they aspire to be. It is the role of the coach to help the client to recognise, clarify and take conscious steps to fulfil their desire to be or become that person. Each time this second iteration of self is remembered, the client can reorientate, balance, rejuvenate and more clearly move towards the direction they desire to take. This is the impulse that motivates the client to make conscious and sustained changes and develop.

Remembering the 'self in potential' offers the client a chance to recall:

- what is truly important and fulfilling
- a clearer sense of direction
- how to reorientate, rebalance and refresh
- the desire and motivation to change and develop.

It is the work of the coach to remain conscious of the importance of these two selves, and to help to guide the client to remember and realise their own source of power, potential and deepening authenticity. In discovering the masterful coach we become aware of the art of helping the client to remember both these iterations of self.

RECOGNISING THE 'SELF IN POTENTIAL'

Often we think that coaching is entirely focused on helping the client to perform better. This is indeed a part of the outcome, but this is just the tip of the iceberg. Coaching is about remembering and recognising the 'self in potential' that we forget – this is the source of your power to help your clients. The coach learns how to remember and visualise potentiality, recalling the prospects and possibilities that await the clients.

To help to illustrate just how powerful the two selves are in coaching, I would like to share an extract from a conversation I had with a senior executive as our coaching work was drawing to a close. Read carefully how this client speaks about his experience of coaching in terms of different selves:

Coach:	What changes have you observed through the coaching?
Client:	It's been an awakening of myself (*pause*) . . . that's been one of the important results for me. The book is not yet finished. We are at the end of the beginning.

Note how he speaks of an awakened self and uses 'the end of the beginning' to describe this enigmatic concept.

Coach:	You're becoming a poet (*smile*).
Client:	I connect a lot more than I did. I don't profess to know myself. I'm also genuinely OK with not knowing the answer. The answer is not it. It's the journey of getting to the answer that it's all about. I realise that now.
Coach:	How do you experience this awakening of the self?
Client:	It's not all about goals, becoming the next CEO or promotion. It's more about discovering a greater sense of self and how I interact. Those

are the really valuable things. It's not only about financial gain, it's more how I relate and can empathise with the question: what can I do for mankind? This involves an investment of self. Previously I did not have a strong voice for myself. I also used to be afraid of being on my own. Now I realise that it's important to be alone and to have my own space and to take time to truly get to know myself. Before I was not committed to what I wanted.

Though performance is an important aspect of coaching and, often, how we frame our interventions, what the client acknowledges primarily is the discovery of a greater sense of self and relationship, together with a clearer sense of purpose.

Coach: And now?

Client: Yes, I'm committed and clearer. I have much greater freedom within to remember what I truly want. This frees me to be in relationships more. I do feel happier and also somehow more fulfilled.

Note how happiness and a sense of fulfilment are two coaching products.

THE 'WHAT' AND THE 'WHY' OF COACHING

In exploring the 'why' of coaching we can see and find important clues to the missing aspects of the 'what'. Only when we remember why we coach do we recognise the true meaning of coaching as a journey. When combined, the 'what' and 'why' of coaching give clues to the nature and source of masterful practice. When we marry the 'what' with the 'why', we realise fundamentally how coaching can facilitate an identity shift. The client can move from a partial concept of self (first self) to experience a more complete, whole and original self (second self).

Chapter Three

THE VISION OF THE COACH

· · ·

Now we will examine the characteristics of the analytical, appreciative and creative eyes and consider how each represents different stages of the evolving vision of the coach. The creative eye combines the analytical and appreciative aspects to give an unlimited 3D vision with an individual, relational and universal awareness. This is the eye employed by the masterful coach.

· · ·

How do we learn to see our own potentiality and that of the client? In wishing to find a coach the client wants to learn how to expand their vision, discover new choices and move closer towards their potential. To facilitate this the coach must already have, and recognise, the importance of an expanded vision. To illustrate how we might learn to expand our vision, let me share with you a model of the three eyes of the coach that has emerged from my own practice.

When I coach I realise that I employ three quite different ways of seeing: an analytical eye, the appreciative eye and the creative eye. These three eyes appear to be distinct and separate. More accurately, they represent key milestones in discovering the evolving vision of the masterful coach, as we will explore.

• MIRADORS •

Each eye looks from a different viewpoint. It may be quite a revelation to realise that our vision of reality is not fixed but can profoundly change depending on the particular viewpoint we take. Not appreciating this conundrum can profoundly limit how we see and practice. Let me explain this more clearly by using an analogy of how I imagine these different viewpoints to be.

I am blessed to spend a good deal of my time in the mountains of Andalucia in southern Spain. The scenery is dramatic and beautiful and the way of living is simple and natural. One of my favourite roads is the road to Ronda, the nearest town to the village where I stay. This road is always an adventure. What I enjoy most are the Spanish miradors. A mirador in the Spanish language is literally a look-out or a viewpoint. As you travel along this road you are invited to stop and visit the different viewing points. I have two particular favourites. One is close to the start of my journey and overlooks the village where I stay. When I stop and visit this viewpoint, I can focus on the activities and changes of the village and explore from above the things that I miss when spending time within it.

The second mirador close to my heart is a stop nearer to my destination. In contrast to the first, this mirador has a panoramic vista. When I look out from this viewpoint my awareness seems to expand. I feel somehow closer to the mountains and can catch a glimpse of the distant Mediterranean. Sometimes I can see even further beyond to a point approximately 100 km away and the distant silhouette of the Atlas Mountains of the continent of Africa.

I value both of these miradors equally and always take time to stop and look. They are contrasting in what they offer the observer. The first is a chance to bring the whole village into focus and to clarify and study how it is changing. The second offers a chance to expand my awareness, to open and look beyond the confines of a more limited field of vision.

Similar to the miradors, the three illustrative eyes that comprise my vision as a coach offer the opportunity to adopt three contrasting viewpoints. Consciously moving between these viewpoints offers the coach profoundly different ways of seeing reality and how we relate. I am mindful when exploring these different viewpoints of not creating a bias to any particular one. Each has its own place and purpose and both serve and limit the vision of the coach, as we will now explore.

• THE ANALYTICAL EYE •

The analytic picture of the human mind is a deterministic machine which, in order to know, isolates objects and events ... such actions are uninformed by the whole.

Peter Senge

In our everyday life and work we mostly employ an analytical eye. This eye belongs to that aspect of you that is fundamentally concerned with protection and survival. The goal of this eye is to offer security and to affirm and strengthen your identity.

VIEWPOINT AND CHARACTERISTICS

VIEWPOINT OF THE ANALYTICAL EYE

This eye takes the viewpoint of a detached observer. It is a clear, cold, objective and scrutinising vision of the visible and physical. When we take this viewpoint we step outside things, taking an exterior view. We look at everything from a position of being on the outside looking in, isolate ourselves and become a part separate from the whole.

The analytical eye seems compelled to look outwardly for the answer. The 'something more' that we seek outside ourselves, and believe will make us complete, is conceived by the analytical eye. This answer may be a bigger and better job, car, house or a more suitable partner.

CHARACTERISTICS OF THE ANALYTICAL EYE

The analytical eye strengthens your personal identity by defining how you are different and distinct. It is a judging eye that believes it has the right answer. Listen carefully to your everyday conversations and you will hear just how much you affirm your personal power and correctness.

The analytical eye seeks problems and provides solutions. It takes a critical, cynical and negative view of things. It is quick and incisive to judge, and is driven to rationalise, process and interpret information. This is the determined and meticulous eye of the perfectionist. In judging right from wrong, it splits the good from the bad – selecting the good and rejecting the bad. It is therefore a divisive eye creating a dualistic vision of reality. It conceives conflict both within and without.

The vision of the analytical eye is one-dimensional (1D) monochromatic – black and white, selecting either this or that. This vision is partial and limited and cannot accommodate both this *and* that.

IMAGINING THE ANALYTICAL EYE

While writing this chapter I taught the three eyes to a group of coaches who wished to extend their practice. While presenting the analytical eye, I asked the group to consider what images might best capture its characteristics. One I liked particularly was the eye of a Sherlock Holmes figure; someone with a big looking glass, always searching for clues and ultimately judging who should or should not be sent to jail.

I was in Amsterdam with my camera and thinking about how prevalent the analytical eye is in everyday life and work. I found myself facing a shop window and took the infrared photograph shown in Figure 5 (p. 34). This image captures the cool rationality of the analytical eye. We look at the world only from our heads and in our busy outward search for the answer can become habitual and quite robotic. This eye has very little or no capacity to self-reflect and so creates a partial 'spectacled' view of reality.

DEVALUING INNER EXPERIENCE

When working with groups as a team coach, it is not uncommon that I am approached at break time by one or more of the participants, with the plea: 'Andrew, please no touchy

Figure 5

feely stuff.' If the analytical eye was to speak its mind then this is what it would say. This eye needs certainty and is very uncomfortable with subjective experience, which raises a particularly important point: the analytical eye has very little or no interior view to its vision. The analytical eye is blind to, and devalues, the inner world of subjective experiences. In its need to know, this eye rationalises and rejects the inner world of experience, including deeper feelings and emotions, values, aspirations and qualities. It is driven by fear rather than being willing to face this emotion.

PAUSE POINT

How does the analytical eye serve and limit your coaching practice?

HOW THE ANALYTICAL EYE SERVES

- It provides a sense of security and certainty – 'a reality check'.
- It offers clear, factual and coherent explanations.
- It simplifies and makes life easier by judging and solving complexity and contradiction.
- It focuses and clarifies.
- It is an efficient eye.
- It is precise and a meticulous eye for detail.
- It is quick to process by rationalising, analysing and interpreting.
- It simplifies by sorting and selecting from multiple data.
- It is a reliable deductive eye that employs reason and logic to extrapolate and formulate.
- It is well informed by memory and can repeatedly draw solutions from the past.

- It informs of the material and physical reality of things – the facts.

The analytical eye provides a sense of security and certainty

When the analytical eye is used in combination with the other eyes, it offers the coach essential skills. Such skills are evident in the above list and include the ability of the coach to focus, clarify and meticulously observe. If, however, the analytical eye is employed alone, its vision can profoundly inhibit your capacity and ability to coach. The following list of limitations clearly indicate why this is so.

HOW THE ANALYTICAL EYE LIMITS

- It is a directive and instructive eye that is comfortable to challenge and debate.
- It is fixed and rigid.
- It is an exclusive eye that is unable to accept another's viewpoint without strong persuasion.
- It is compulsive and fast to process.
- It interprets only a limited field of data, namely the visible and factual.
- It is concerned more with the quantity of things and ignores the quality of experience.
- It differentiates, isolating the part from the whole.
- It has little or no capacity to reflect or relate.
- It is a judging eye that is divisive and dualistic.
- It oversimplifies complexity, offering a reductive and one-sided solution.
- It is the infallible eye of the perfectionist.

- It is politically motivated and seeks not only the absolute truth, but also the one right answer and way of doing things.
- It fears being emotionally overwhelmed.

Let us consider some of the key points from this list to illustrate how using the analytical eye alone can limit your capacity to coach.

THE COMPULSION TO ANSWER RATHER THAN QUESTION

The temptation of the analytical eye is to provide the answer rather than to question. The way you can recognise a domineering analytical eye is when you feel the need to provide the answer to your clients, rather than allowing them, through your questions, to discover their own. Providing the answer steals the chance for clients to solve their own issues and challenges. Personally owning the issue and recognising the desire to change are key realisations within the coaching experience. Essentially the coaching relationship provides clients with the opportunity to learn about their inner resourcefulness.

THE NEED TO RATIONALISE RATHER THAN RELATE

By overlooking the interior world of subjective experience, the analytical eye is compelled to rationalise and is unable to empathise and relate. Fundamentally, coaching is a relationship through which the coach learns how to understand the needs and desires of clients and helps them to take conscious steps towards fulfilling them. It is essential that the coach learns the importance of empathy. The continuous temptation to rationalise inhibits this prospect.

INFALLIBILITY – OVERLOOKING THE POTENTIAL VALUE OF PROBLEMS

The analytical is the eye of the perfectionist. When a problem is seen it is quickly solved. Problems are judged to be unwanted, the goal is their solution. To the analytical eye a problem without an answer is a failing. From this viewpoint, the problem is not considered in any way to be a possible source of potential learning for the client or key to their growth and development.

POLITICS AND DISEMPOWERMENT

The analytical eye believes it has the right answer. This view creates a strong political stance where individuals believe there is just one right and tested way of doing things – 'my way'. When this position is asserted, the chance for others to engage and find their own solution is taken away. Such a political stance can stifle the very thing it wishes to foster – the creativity and motivation of a more productive workforce. The standpoint of a strong analytical eye is likely to disempower and disengage the clients, stealing away their chance to realise their own inner resourcefulness. Once more, this sense of knowing the right way of doings things and having the answer can profoundly limit the prospect of successful coaching.

NOT SEEING BLINDNESS TO HOW WE REACT

We have already explored how, in judging right from wrong, the analytical eye selects what it sees as correct and rejects what it deems as wrong. Such judging splits and divides our sense of self, banishing the bad to the edge of our consciousness. Ultimately we can never truly banish these rejected parts as they will seek to be remembered through the unconscious and subjective experience. The analytical eye is blind to this and is completely unaware of how our own unconscious reactions can strongly influence and impact on how we relate, including in the coaching relationship.

SLEEPING BEAUTY

While writing this chapter, I was invited to a performance of the ballet *Sleeping Beauty*. As the orchestra played the enchanting score, I recalled a childhood memory. I once had an orange vinyl record that I and my twin brother endlessly played. It told the story of Sleeping Beauty in words and music. Although this was over forty years ago, as specific parts of the musical score were played, words and even sentences from the story came back into my mind. At one point, laughing to myself, I quoted a whole sentence – to the dismissive stare of my friend sitting next to me.

I became immersed in the dancing and stage play and how the different characters were portrayed. I looked around at the packed audience in this magnificent theatre and wondered: why does this ballet have such universal appeal? Maybe we are all 'sleeping beauties'? The analytical eye, in wishing to protect and define us, is unable to see inside and experience our inner beauty. Might we then live a good deal of our lives only partially awake? Is there a danger that we, too, may sleep for a hundred years? More importantly, how might we awake from our sleep?

> The analytical eye, by building our sense of security and identity, isolates us from our wholeness, providing a very disconnected view of reality

I am drawn at this point to the words of Albert Einstein, who recognised that we suffer an optical 'delusion':

> There is an optical delusion of consciousness where we
> experience ourselves as something separate from the
> rest. We are invited to widen our circle of compassion to
> embrace all living creatures and the whole of nature in
> its beauty.

In seeking the comfort of what is certain and known, we appear to disconnect ourselves from the whole and suffer a partial and limited vision. It is the partiality of the vision of the analytical eye that profoundly limits your ability to coach.

• THE APPRECIATIVE EYE •

The second eye of the coach is the appreciative eye (Figure 6, opposite). This offers a markedly different vision of reality that contrasts with that of the analytical eye, as described below.

VIEWPOINT AND CHARACTERISTICS

VIEWPOINT OF THE APPRECIATIVE EYE

The appreciative eye adopts the position and viewpoint of an inner observer that looks at reality from the inside out. It is comfortable to simply experience rather than process and analyse. The appreciative eye is a sensing eye that can develop awareness by attuning to the sensations of the body. This offers the coach a capacity to listen inwardly so that our vision can be expanded to sense feelings, values, aspirations, passions and qualities. In contrast to the analytical eye, the appreciative eye can recognise our inner resourcefulness and begins the exploration of how we can discover and access the source of our hidden potential.

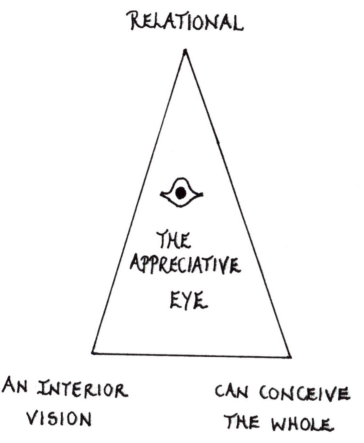

Figure 6

CHARACTERISTICS OF THE APPRECIATIVE EYE

Rather than seeking to answer, the appreciative eye is a curious eye that is comfortable to question. It is patient and reflective. Its motivation is to understand and appreciate. This eye offers a fresh view of reality that we associate with the beginner's mind. The opening of this eye marks another milestone of the journey in awakening the vision of the masterful coach.

The appreciative eye offers a capacity to listen inwardly

This eye is encouraging and supportive. It focuses on the positive core of individuals, affirming their strengths. Through this eye we are able to extend our vision beyond oneself to encompass a wider appreciation and understanding of others. This is the nature of how we relate with empathy. With the capacity to embrace both self and other, the appreciative eye offers the coach a two-dimensional (2D) vision.

The appreciative eye is comfortable with seeing beyond the visible and factual. It is sensitive to inner motivations, aspirations and qualities. The appreciative eye has an integrative vision and seeks to conceive of the larger whole in which we are a part. This is the bigger context that, when realised, can give our life deeper meaning. This eye is comfortable to look for the 'something more' beyond the material. Rather than return to the memories of the past to inform how we act, this eye is able to conceive and contemplate the prospect of the future and all its possibilities as a potential source of learning.

IMAGINING THE APPRECIATIVE EYE

When I imagine the experience of opening the appreciative eye, I see a doorway similar to the one shown in Figure 7 (opposite). As the appreciative eye opens, so does an inner doorway through which we are invited to step and to experience our interior world. This is an enterprising eye that is comfortable to take the risk of stepping beyond the rational and what is known and certain. It deepens our understanding of self and other and how we relate.

Figure 7

PAUSE POINT

Consider how the appreciative eye serves and limits your coaching practice.

HOW THE APPRECIATIVE EYE SERVES

- It is a relational, patient and empathic eye.
- It is an accepting and inclusive eye.
- It is an enterprising, reflective and curious eye that is comfortable to question.
- It is an integrative eye that conceives the larger context of things, the whole and how we fit in.
- It sees the positive core and seeks to discover an individual's strengths, achievements and continuing success.
- It is a sensing and qualitative eye that can attune to the interior world of subjective experience.

THE CAPACITY TO RELATE RATHER THAN RATIONALISE

The appreciative eye is keen to relate rather than rationalise. Though we often talk of the work of the coach in singular terms, coaching depends on the dynamic of the coaching *relationship*. The primary intention of the coach is to be able to relate sufficiently to understand the needs of their clients and to help them to remember their innate desires and motivation to change. This realisation is vital to the work of the coach.

THE ABILITY TO QUESTION RATHER THAN ANSWER

Whereas the analytical eye is swift to answer, the appreciative eye offers the coach the ability and capacity to question. Rather than seeking to know for certain, this eye is quite comfortable to sense and explore. The art of questioning lies at the heart of coaching. Guided and supported by the coach, clients are invited to reflect and to expand their awareness.

DEVELOPING EMOTIONAL AWARENESS

In its ability to sense and experience the subjective, the appreciative eye offers the coach a deepening emotional awareness and intelligence. The appreciative eye is a feeling eye. Whereas the analytical eye fears and rejects 'the touchy feely stuff', the appreciative eye is curious and able to meet with, own and explore our emotions, values, aspirations and passions. The appreciative eye seeks to accommodate these experiences as the basis of how we relate, and can more deeply understand the self and others. Whereas the analytical eye judges our emotions to be our enemies, the appreciative eye seeks and values emotions as our closest friends.

As the coach awakens the appreciative eye, the bridge between feelings and thoughts is reinstated, together with the integration of the head and heart. Now emotions can guide and influence thought, offering us the ability to reorientate and respond.

HOW THE APPRECIATIVE EYE LIMITS

- It is a spontaneous and unstructured eye.
- It lacks form and solid substance.
- It is an expansive eye that opens things up rather than closes them down.
- It is a qualitative and irrational eye.
- It is an emotive eye.
- It is concerned with the quality of how we relate.

- It favours reflection to discrete action.
- It is an eye that has depth and breadth, but is lacking in focus and clarity.

WITHOUT FORM AND STRUCTURE

The major limitation of the appreciative eye is in its lack of form and structure. It is a reflective eye that is expansive and seeks the larger context to our working lives. In the coaching dynamic, the conscious expansion of awareness is ideally balanced by a conscious contraction – a focusing, distilling and processing of information. The appreciative eye alone cannot achieve this. Only when this eye is combined with others can the perceptions of the appreciative eye be grounded and informed. The appreciative eye can deeply relate and build awareness, yet it lacks the structure and focus necessary to bring clarity and to make meaning of our experience. This possibility is realised with the opening of the creative eye, as we will now explore.

• THE CREATIVE EYE •

The point of arrival we realise is our original point of departure.

Piero Ferruci

Let us examine how the characteristics of the analytical and appreciative eyes are markedly different when compared. In the following list, can you see how the limitations of one correspond directly to the strengths of the other? This gives an important clue to their true interrelationship. Rather than viewing these eyes as separate and distinct, can we instead combine them as if they were the two sides of the same coin? Might we then consider how the composite eye could further evolve the vision of the coach? This more creative eye would offer a dynamic three-dimensional (3D) vision.

ANALYTICAL	APPRECIATIVE
Outer observer	Inner observer
Exterior view	Interior view
Objective	Subjective
Detached	Relational
Problem solving	Experiencing
Sees partiality	Sees wholeness
Impartial	Empathic
Seeing	Sensing
Thinking	Feeling
Incisive	Expansive
Focused	Reflective
Active	Receptive
Reactive	Responsive
Quantitative	Qualitative
Facts	Experience
Rational	Irrational
Superficial	Depth
Negative	Positive
Planned	Spontaneous
Critical	Valuing
Judging	Encouraging
Dispassionate	Passionate
Black or white	Subtle – shades of grey
One-dimensional	Two-dimensional
Problem seeking	Strength and success affirming
Scientific approach	Artistic approach
Differentiating	Integrating
Past focus	Future focus
Self-affirming	Self-effacing

The creative eye accommodates the joint strengths of the appreciative and analytical while compensating their individual limitation. This creative eye offers both the reflective capacity to expand awareness and the focus to clarify. An illustration of the interrelationship of the three eyes of coaching is given in Figure 8, below.

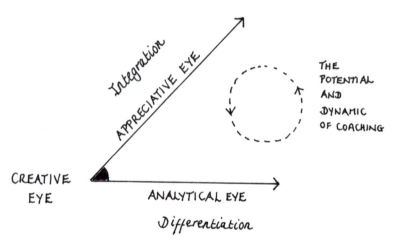

Figure 8

VIEWPOINT AND CHARACTERISTICS

VIEWPOINT OF THE CREATIVE EYE

I named this the creative eye because it connects us to our origin and source. In discovering this viewpoint we realise a deeper centre of identity – the source from which our values, aspirations and qualities originate. We can access our hidden potential and utilise our inner resources as the desire and motivation to make sustained changes. The coach can then become a responsive and conscious co-creator of the client's most ideal future.

The creative eye is multidimensional. It is not fixed, but flexible

The creative eye is dynamic and multidimensional. Its viewpoint is not fixed but flexible. It is able, at will, to adopt several viewpoints where reality is seen subjectively and objectively, accommodating both an interior and exterior, and an individual and collective vision of reality.

CHARACTERISTICS OF THE CREATIVE EYE

The creative eye balances the compulsion to answer and process information, with the patience and choice to question and empathically relate. Whereas the analytical eye is often reactive and the appreciative eye receptive, the creative eye is truly responsive. This eye offers a deep and intimate understanding and appreciation of yourself and your client.

The creative eye can both integrate and differentiate, and, therefore, potentially synthesise. This eye may recall historical memories of the past or, equally, conceive of new and novel future possibilities. Through the dynamic vision of the creative eye, past and future are brought together into conscious awareness through the portal of the present moment. This offers the coach the potential of a much more unlimited vision and the freedom to respond. This dynamic flexibility and responsiveness can free us to discover the masterful coach.

> What makes the creative eye unique is its ability to realise and bring into form and express our wholeness as well as our partiality

This is essential to allow us to make conscious the meaning and value of the larger energetic field in which we participate. What we can then realise is the ideal future we desire. Equally, as we will explore more fully later in this text, we remember and rediscover our most natural, truest and genuine self – our original self.

IMAGINING OF THE CREATIVE EYE

Seeking a photographic image that symbolises the creative eye, I have been repeatedly drawn back to recall a short stay in the Lake District of northern England. While walking around one of the beautiful lakes of this area, my peace and mind had stilled and I was simply observing the wonder of this truly natural setting and scenery. The lake is one of nature's great mirrors and is one of the places to which I return to reflect. On this day it seemed to offer a picture of everything in perfect symmetry and balance. The vast majesty of the ancient mountains seemed to be present and in the moment. My future wishes and aspirations, in this same moment, felt possible, even probable. In the stillness and reflection of the lake, nothing seemed impossible or out of reach (Figure 9, opposite).

The creative eye, not unlike the image shown in Figure 9, is deeply reflective. It has a truly expansive vision and a capacity to focus and discern in meticulous detail. This is a patient and responsive eye that can bring the past and future to their conscious conclusion in the fullness of the present moment. It offers a single point to which we can return and from which we can balance, while remembering the source of our innate motivation for change. Such is the possibility and prospect of masterful coaching.

At my best, in moments of mastery, I imagine I am coaching from the very moorings of the little boat: observing, reflecting, listening and imagining what may be happening in the depths of myself and my clients. I am intimately seeking to relate and to understand my clients deeply and help to guide them in taking responsibility and making the sustained changes they desire. The coach then becomes a co-creator.

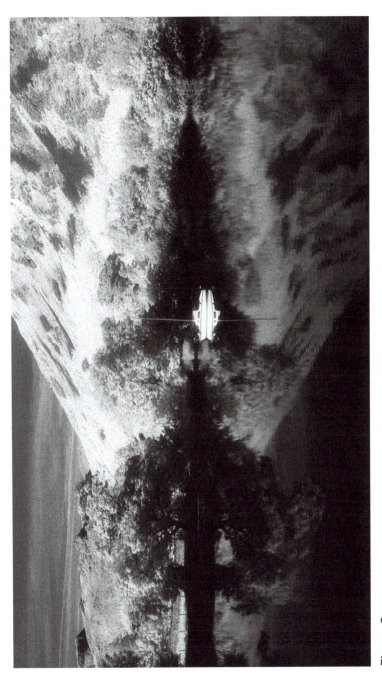

Figure 9

> ## PAUSE POINT
>
> **Consider if the creative eye can offer you masterful practice. How can it do this?**

REALISING A MORE UNLIMITED VISION

How can the creative eye serve your practice as a coach?

- It allows you to balance and reorientate yourself.
- It is a patient and playful eye.
- It is a truly responsive eye that operates by making choices.
- It can question and help to answer, and also invite you to sit with the unanswered question.
- By helping you to reflect, focus and relate, this eye can expand awareness and clarify current reality.
- It is an accepting and compassionate eye.
- It has 3D vision, including an interior and exterior, an individual and collective, and a universal dimension.
- It can resource the past and future within the present moment.
- It is sensitive to, and can discern, unconscious reaction.
- It is happy to reflect on the meaning of complexity and contradiction, without an urgency to solve.
- It can embrace and resolve conflict.
- It offers the discovery of a creative originality.

DEVELOPING PSYCHOLOGICAL AWARENESS

This sensitivity of the creative eye cultivates an in-depth psychological awareness that is initiated with the opening of the appreciative eye. Here the coach can begin to sense and separate the impact and influence of their own psychology from that of their clients. Distractions can be inwardly minimised. This refines the vision and deepens the sensitivity of the coach and their practice, as we will illustrate later in the book.

DISCERNING HOW WE REACT

In stark contrast to the analytical eye, the appreciative eye can sense the interior world of subjective experience. The creative eye can take this one step further and discern how we react. This eye has the insight, subtlety and sensitivity to be able to separate how we react from how we respond. It has the capacity to be able to spot our own reactions and the reactions of others. It can reintegrate those parts we label as bad by bringing them back into our conscious awareness and control. The coach can now help their clients to own and tell their untold stories that may have been continually repeated and played out on others. This capacity to discern how we react allows us to acknowledge reaction and make choices of how we wish to respond. In this way the coach can help to transform reaction into response. This refines and heightens our ability to relate and coach.

RESOLVING CONFLICT

The creative eye is deeply self-reflective. This allows the coach to contemplate and see beyond the need to judge. The conflict of 'either this or that' is embraced and considered, with space for something more still to emerge. This eye can hold opposing and conflicting possibilities, without the temptation to process or reductively problem-solve. It sees reality as it is, without a need to react or analyse. This eye can accept – and will attentively listen to – both sides of the argument.

> The creative eye can see conflict without judgement; it is unconditional and compassionate

REALISING A MORE UNLIMITED VISION

As we will explore more fully in Chapter 6, through the vision of the creative eye we discover the masterful coach. For now and in summary, it is important to realise that the emergence of the creative eye brings with it the combined strengths of both the analytical and appreciative eyes. It has a much more unlimited vision, together with a deepening capacity to relate.

• THE THREE EYES IN PRACTICE •

In addition to working as a coach, I also take a special interest in coaching other coaches and helping to develop and continually deepen their practice. To illustrate how the three different eyes of the coach are employed in practice, let me share with you two recent case studies. The first is a coaching client who needed to develop an appreciative eye. The second illustrates how an experienced coach continues to evolve her vision and practice through discovering the creative eye.

AWAKENING THE APPRECIATIVE EYE

Peter is a senior manager and leader. A number of people from his department have complained to Human Resources (HR) that Peter is not giving them the support they need. Peter begins coaching feeling undermined and unclear of what may be happening in his department. The following are excerpts taken from coaching sessions that show how Peter awakens the appreciative eye from the baseline of a strong analytical vision and discovers the impact of his previous blindness.

Coach: Tell me about the issue you face, Peter.

Peter: A couple of people in my department have complained about me and gone behind my back to HR.

Coach: What was your experience of what happened?

Peter: One of the persons in question came to me with a problem. There were things going on that I didn't understand. He told me a little about his issues. I wanted to help him and so told him what to do.

Here Peter's strong analytical eye is present. He believes that his answer to what he thinks is the problem will satisfy his staff and is the best way to help others.

Coach: You told him what to do?

Peter: Yes, he was telling me about his challenges and so I told him what would help to solve them. I shared the way I would do it with him.

Coach: How much do you care about your staff, Peter?

Peter: This really matters to me. I really do want to help them. I am always thinking, what can I do to help? And I tell them what to do, what I would do.

Note how much Peter truly does care and is keen to help his staff. From the viewpoint of the analytical eye, the best way of helping is seen to be by giving the right answer.

Coach: I can see how much you care, but I wonder if your staff realise just how much you do feel and care?

Peter:	What do you mean? I do care a great deal.
Coach:	I know you do (*pause*). When people come to you they may not present you with the real issue at first. They test if they can trust you – if you can relate and appreciate what's happening to them. If you allow them to tell their story, their trust in you builds. They may then tell you what is really happening. My question, Peter, is: are you able to see this person without wanting to solve his problem?
Peter:	Mmm – I want to help and I do care.
Coach:	Shall we try to act this out between us, Peter? Let me play the member of staff and you be the boss – play yourself.

We step into roles.

Peter:	OK.
Coach:	Hi, Peter. I've got something going on.
Peter:	What is it and can I help?
Coach:	Yes, maybe. I'm really struggling with something.
Peter:	Is it personal?
Coach:	Sort of.
Peter:	You know, we have a good counselling support service in this company if you need personal help.
Coach:	Mmm. I have problem with workload and it's effecting home as well at the moment.

I am sensing in this role-play that something is stopping me bringing in how I am feeling – that it would be somehow wrong to do so. If I can't express how I feel and be acknowledged by Peter without judgement, then I can't trust the situation enough to say what is really happening.

Peter:	OK, why don't you talk with your immediate line manager and we can explore your workload?
Coach:	Mmm. Peter, can I come out of role and speak to you about my experience? First, how was that for you?
Peter:	I really wanted to help you. Anything that I could do, I wanted to help.
Coach:	Can I be frank about my experience so that we can work this through together?
Peter:	Yes please.
Coach:	I could see you wanted to help, but you weren't helping me. There was so much more that I wanted to say to you about my problem, but, because you were offering me your solutions, something in me felt shut down. I didn't feel you empathised and really wanted to know how I felt. But I did see that you really wanted to help and were happy to offer me your solution.
Peter:	Really? Might that be why some of my folks are going behind my back to Human Resources?
Coach:	What do you think?
Peter:	Maybe.
Coach:	And what is missing that you are not valuing or offering, Peter?
Peter:	I'm not good with feelings or emotions. I'm a very practical and pragmatic man.
Coach:	Tell me about emotions and feelings.
Peter:	I'm not sure how to deal with emotions. A bit scared really.

The analytical eye sees emotions as the unknown and often fears them.

Coach:	I could sense this – when I was in role it felt you were scared of mine too, which didn't allow me to tell you how I was feeling or what was really going on.
Peter:	Really? I do want to help by offering my best solutions but in fact I'm actually doing the opposite – aren't I?
Coach:	Yes. That may be true. Tell me, what do you think you have been missing?
Peter:	Giving my staff a chance to say how it really is and being able to listen and hear them without offering my solution.

Note how Peter realises that there is another way – through opening the appreciative eye he has a non-judging, more empathic and relational viewpoint.

Coach:	Exactly. Maybe because you don't place a value on feelings as much as answers and solutions, you are unknowingly devaluing them. This is not a judgement, Peter, but a perception.
Peter:	Damn. I do want to help and in fact I'm doing the opposite.
Coach:	It's a perception that would be valuable for you to work with. Are you willing to do that? To see how you might approach this differently and to explore if this may bring about a very different response from your staff?
Peter:	Yes. I need to. Yes I'm willing to do that.

Peter was able to explore his emotions and feelings more fully in the sessions that followed. Each morning before work he would walk his dog and use this time to reflect about his learning and key aspects of life and work. Peter brought a key change into the next session.

Coach: Let's check in, Peter. How are you today?

Peter: I'm OK. Things are moving along. I'm working on a key change initiative.

Despite the good news about the key piece of work, I see a real sadness in Peter's eyes and sense heaviness in his energy. I decide to explore this further.

Coach: You look a little sad and down. What's going on Peter? Are you OK to speak about it?

Peter: I feel a little depressed and quite stuck. I think I've been stuck for a while.

Peter is owning and openly expressing his emotions.

Coach: Thank you, Peter, for being able to include this. I have been wondering how you truly feel.

Peter: It's not a good place to be. I don't allow myself to be here often.

Coach: I know that (*pause*), but might there be value in being here? Just in being willing to say how it is and how you feel? Your emotions may be friends and helpful in some way if you are simply willing to include them.

Peter: I feel stuck in a groove. I don't feel I've been treated well. People don't seem to care enough. I haven't been supported in the way I deserve. I've been hurt by what's happened.

Coach:	I really hear that, Peter, and can see how important this is and how it's affected you.
Peter:	I've been running away from this.
Coach:	Yes, I see. It seems very real when you tell me how it is for you – how you truly feel. I then feel a strong connection with you, Peter, a very strong connection.

I am mirroring how his willingness to share is emotions has made Peter more real, and our relationship has deepened as a result.

Peter:	I hadn't realised how much I've been running and hiding from this.
Coach:	And yet this, your experience, is important and real. How might I help you, Peter?
Peter:	In a way it's just good to let myself speak like this, and then I know how I feel.
Coach:	How important are your feelings to you?
Peter:	Very.
Coach:	How come?
Peter:	They help me to understand myself and where I am. Otherwise I don't know where I am. Having spoken about them I feel somehow free to move on – a little, at least.
Coach:	What an interesting learning (*pause*).
Peter:	What do you mean?
Coach:	You are valuing your emotions and experience. Can we go full circle?
Peter:	Sure.
Coach:	What happened when your staff came to you?
Peter:	Oh I see (*pause*). Maybe they need what just happened here.

Coach:	Well, how do you feel right now?
Peter:	I feel seen and understood. I feel accepted and more real and quite still and solid.
Coach:	What if I had offered you a solution instead?
Peter:	I think I might have felt angry and overlooked.
Coach:	There it is Peter (*pause*). What are you taking away from this realisation into your work?
Peter:	I'm going to try to listen for people's feelings more and also allow space for their feelings as well as my own. They may be scary but they make me real and help me to relate.
Coach:	Do you feel able to do that now?
Peter:	Yes, I'll try it. I may get caught in solving again, but I now know how it feels when I simply give my answers to others.

At the next session Peter has found himself working with an external consultant who has evaluated a course on which Peter teaches. This consultant is bullish and dictating to Peter and his colleagues how things need to change.

Peter:	I found myself listening to this man and saying to myself: have you no idea how much you are disengaging this group and making them very angry? Yet he was totally blind to what was going on. All he wanted to do was to tell them his assessment, how he saw things.
Coach:	Isn't that strange that you should meet such a man (*smiling*)?
Peter:	Yes. I see what you are saying (*laughs*), when I think of my personal journey. And it's me that's

dealing with it and trying to mirror back to this man his blindness. If he expects the group to work with him then he has to realise the impact of his own behaviour and how it's made the group feel. How he has imposed his views without accommodating any of ours (*pause*) Andrew, I am becoming a facilitator!

Coach: I realise that and you are being asked to teach what you have learned.

Peter: Would you believe it?

Coach: What's it like to be a facilitator?

Note how the role of facilitator is from a place of choice: it is a non-judging viewpoint where Peter can appreciate and express both sides. It's the view from the appreciative and creative eyes.

Peter: I feel free that I can stand outside things, even when I am part of things. I don't get caught like I used to – forcing my own opinions and solutions on others. I'm quite happy now to observe and think about what difference I can make. I don't have to be in control. I can choose to act rather than simply react. Here this man was reacting and I could see the damage he was doing in telling us the solution, and he was completely blind to it.

Coach: In your awareness, you have come a long way Peter.

THE CREATIVE EYE OF THE COACH IN PRACTICE

Susan is a qualified, experienced and practising coach. These excerpts are taken directly from two consecutive coaching supervision sessions where Susan was keen to explore some of the edges of her practice in order to continue to learn and grow.

Susan: I love 'doing'.

Whenever I hear about 'doing things' I recognise the analytical eye and its need to get things done – to find the answer, to process and solve.

Coach: How does doing serve you?

Susan: When I do things I feel as though I have achieved something. I get more satisfaction from doing. I can see what I've done. Often I feel as though I have to do things. I'll watch television to relax but often feel guilty for not doing things. Moving is vital to me – I have to be on the move and doing things.

Coach: Anything more?

Susan: This keeps me busy, I feel as though I'm getting somewhere. Sometimes, particularly around the guilt thing when I'm watching TV, I think that doing is something I should do. There is voice that tells me that doing is a must.

Coach: Whose voice is that?

Note how the voices of judgement, fear and cynicism are closely associated with the analytical eye. When we employ this eye the inner voices – which tell us what we should and must do – are never far away.

Susan: Mmm. I'm not sure. It's been with me a long time.

Coach: Yes. I wonder whose expectations they are – that you should do things?

Susan:	It's my strong work ethic. You have to do to achieve. It was probably drummed into me. I'm not good at 'being' because I like to be on the move.
Coach:	And you can only be when you are not moving?
Susan:	So they say. All this meditation stuff, this being, involves stopping. I like to keep on the move. Even when I sit down at home in the evening I sit in a rocking chair and rock.

I realise that a reframe may help here. Rather than splitting 'doing' and 'being' through the dualistic vision of the analytical eye, can Susan expand her vision to see the possibility of experiencing both? Can she extend her vision to see the non-dual reality of the creative eye?

Coach:	Susan, let me plant a seed. When you talk about being and doing you separate the two. Doing is moving, being is still. How would it be to consider a third way? What if your being was in your doing? What if you could find perfect stillness and being within every busy moment?
Susan:	Mmm. So that I'm present in the moment and in all that I do?
Coach:	Yes. It may not be 'either, or' but allowing yourself to experience 'both'
Susan:	Yes. Mmm (*laughing*).
Coach:	Might it not be as black and white as you think?
Susan:	I'm always trying to separate things. So the seed that you plant for me to consider is that being and doing can be one and the same – the being in the doing? Mmm (*pause*).

| Coach: | Yes. Maybe the more we make the being a destiny, the more it becomes out of our reach. What do you think? |
| Susan: | Maybe (*long pause*). Yes. |

At the next session we continued our exploration.

Susan:	From the last session, the thing that keeps coming back to me all the time is what you said about noticing the being in your doing.
Coach:	Yes.
Susan:	I love that. This has been a real 'ah ha' for me. Realising that I can be and do at the same time is wonderful. And I just keep smiling, noticing that I'm doing both. It's incredibly liberating. It's wonderful.
Coach:	Tell me a little more about what your experience is.
Susan:	Erm (*pause*). It's a connectedness, so it's a connection with myself and it's a connection with other people. When we were talking before about being in the moment, I now notice this when I'm with other people and how that manifests. I am not thinking in my head at all. It's more energy, I'm just energy and I just notice things about the other person in a non-judgemental way.

Note the opening of the creative eye here – relational, non-judging, unconditional, with a focus on experience and in-the-moment reality – and also the in-flow experience ('I'm just energy').

| Coach: | Mmm. |

Susan:	But also non-judgemental with me. When I'm not in this place, I'm wondering if this person likes me or if I'm saying the right things. So all of that goes away and I'm just connected with myself (*pause*). It starts as a simple thing. Just noticing my feet on the floor or my bottom on the chair, and then I just think 'Yes, I am here'. It's as simple as that, but then it makes me grin (*smiling*), then I notice that I'm doing it – being it.

Notice that when the creative eye opens, Susan is able to focus on her experiences and this switches off the inner voices that can judge and criticise.

Coach:	(*Smiling*) There's a new conscious awareness in you.
Susan:	Yes (*pause*). Yes.
Coach:	What are you connected to?
Susan:	(*Laughing – long pause*) It's a non-judging connection. It's what it is, a connection – a connectedness.
Coach:	Is this awareness you?
Susan:	Erm, it probably is (*smiles*), it's me without any of my head stuff, so yes it's me – isn't it? It's just me in the world connecting with somebody else in the world; all the assumptions about anything else are all switched off.
Coach:	Is this a more natural you?
Susan:	Yes. It's a purer me. It's everything I'm about, keeping it simple and it's just that simple – a pure smile feeling.

Note how Susan recognises a 'purer' experience – a connection to a deeper more authentic being and self.

Coach: The being that is you, when you are in your
            being (*smiling*).
Susan: Yes, yes (*laughing together*).
Coach: It's strangely paradoxical, and when we both
            laugh it's maybe because we are acknowledging
            a discovery.

*Note how our deeper original self is able to accommodate and accept
paradox as a norm.*

Susan: Well it's so obvious at one level and yet com-
            pletely complicated at another.
Coach: If it's so obvious (*smiling*), I wonder what you
            missed before?
Susan: It's a type of connection that is beyond rapport,
            more like I have found before with animals. It's
            a non-verbal connection – a 'zzzzzzzzzz'.
Coach: Yes (*laughing together*). What's the
            'zzzzzzzzzzzz'?
Susan: Its energy, all your energies line up. There's an
            attraction, like lots of little magnets lining up.
            What I tend to do is to keep people at a distance
            because it's safe. This is more about allowing
            the magnetic thing to happen and simply just
            notice.
Coach: So how does this serve you as a coach?

*Now I am inviting Susan to ground this learning in her work and
practice.*

Susan: I've realised how much I do use this when I
            coach – my smiling bit. I can cut through all
            the stuff to find what's real. It enables me to be

	more authentic and to truly connect and to help my clients do the same.
Coach:	Are you saying that something of this type of connection allows you to be more authentic?
Susan:	Yes, and it gives my clients the same permission.
Coach:	Isn't that interesting?
Susan:	Yes. It's what I do and know that I do it. This is when my coaching is at its best. It can bring about change at an identity level. Andrew, you are able to work here, that is why it almost always brings impact and change.
Coach:	Coaching in the organisational setting is often thought to be about improving performance. You are suggesting that it can be much deeper at an identity level?
Susan:	Yes, that's true.
Coach:	It raises an interesting observation for us to consider – how you might influence more by how you coach than what you do.
Susan:	Yes (*pause*). Yes that's true. When you're experiencing, it's much easier to help your clients to connect with *their* experience. This makes a difference and can often help the coaching to shift.
Coach:	So rather than be caught in processing we are able to acknowledge key experiences, and this somehow helps the client to shift?
Susan:	Yes. I have one client who is very mind identified and always busy. I remember noticing his passion one day. I said 'I notice how passionate you are about this, aren't you?' He replied, 'Yes,

I suppose I am.' This noticing of experiences, feelings and emotions seems to bring about important shifts. He actually stopped and reflected. I suppose this experiencing takes our clients out of their heads for a while. A few sessions ago you said: 'You don't have to say it out loud, but you do need to acknowledge how you feel.' That's an interesting process. It's liberating. The feelings then don't overwhelm, if you're able to own them.

Coach: You're speaking about the importance of allowing yourself to experience without judging and analysing.

Susan notes the power of sensing and experiencing that exists beyond the judging analytical eye.

Susan: Yes.

Chapter Four

THE ESSENTIAL INSTRUMENTS

• • •

In this chapter we will explore how the analytical, appreciative and creative eyes each have a characteristic instrument that is vital to the work of the coach – the lens, mirror and compass, respectively. These are the elements that comprise the essential inner toolkit of the masterful coach.

• • •

Each of the eyes provides a specific instrument that is essential to the work of the coach. By identifying these inner instruments we can better apply each eye in practice and show how, in combination, they can lead to the discovery of mastery. Let us examine each instrument in turn, and its particular role and value to the coach.

• DISCOVERING THE TOOLS OF THE TRADE •

Having decided to become a coach, it is very tempting to immediately begin to try to find 'tools of the trade'. This may include lengthy questionnaires, tools that assess your clients' preferred style, or different coaching models. When I decided to become a coach, I remember asking Joan Roberts, an established coach, whom I admire, 'What is the best coaching model?' I recall, to this day, how Joan drew two circles on a page, with some arrows between and we talked for almost an hour about how people relate. I still have this piece of paper and can openly admit that I never fully understood the model. But keeping the piece of paper brought sufficient calm and confidence for me to continue on the journey of becoming a coach.

While we have to find compassion for the part of us that needs the structure of such models, we are invited to trust that the essential toolkit of the coach is actually very light and, most importantly, does not need to be externally carried.

THE INNER TOOLKIT

Though we automatically look outside for our tools, becoming a masterful coach involves the discovery and cultivation of an inner toolkit.

The search for external tools can disguise the fact that the essential tools of coaching await our discovery within. It is the compulsion of the analytical eye to search outwardly for answers and tools. This, in turn, inhibits what is vital to your coaching – your ability to keep your tools 'light'. By keeping things light, you free yourself up to truly relate and be present in the coaching space with your client. The need to use something specific takes away the chance for you and your client to experience the generative mystery of the coaching relationship. This is not to deny the value of employing some external coaching tools. My suggestion is that we employ these tools specifically and sparingly, while remaining conscious of how they can limit as well as serve the masterful work of the coach.

CLIENTS' EXPECTATIONS

It's not just new coaches that are anxious to gather and use coaching tools: you will find that some clients expect you to bring coaching tools into the frame. The example below demonstrates the scenario you may often confront.

Alan is a very bright senior manager, leader and finance specialist, and is held in high regard with a good deal of responsibility. He works in a major complex multinational organisation. One of the first questions he asked of me in our initial meeting was:

Alan: What tools will you use and bring into the coaching?

Rather than responding immediately by offering a short list of what I might employ, I smiled and said:

Coach: How important do you think tools are?

Alan: Very. They'll give us something to focus on in the coaching. What's your view, Andrew?

Coach: I think tools can get in the way of the true work of the coach, which is to understand you deeply and help you to make the changes that you desire and can commit to make.

My curiosity was engaged and I wondered whether Alan's need for external tools might cover a resistance to developing a coaching relationship, so the next question followed quite naturally.

Coach: How comfortable are you to enter into a coaching relationship right now?

Alan was able to voice a real hesitation about beginning coaching and added a touch of cynicism that we explored together. It was a fruitful discussion that helped him to make conscious his own fears and doubts about the value of coaching – our work together had already begun.

We will now explore in more detail how the essential inner instruments of the coach, individually and collectively, inform our practice and help us to achieve mastery.

• THE LENS •

The lens is the instrument of the analytical eye. Its role is to bring clarity and focus to current reality. This lens processes information by selecting, sorting and analysing. It continually contracts and focuses our field of awareness. Without the lens we would live a blurred existence, never fully in focus.

In the coaching process, the lens plays a vital role in:

- setting and agreeing the expectations and boundaries of the coaching frame;
- clarifying the client's desired goal;
- focusing and selecting what is key and of interest to the client;
- agreeing outcomes and learning;
- identifying the principal choices that clients wish to make and the actions they wish to take.

The full potential and value of the lens to the work of the coach is realised only when it is combined with the other instruments, which we will explore. When it is employed on its own, through the vision of the analytical eye, it allows us to sample only a small portion of the energy field in which we interact and participate – the visible and factual. This confines our vision and all that we may sense beyond the visible, as illustrated in Figure 10, below.

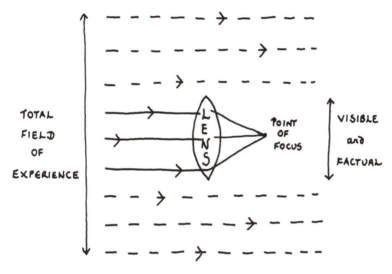

Figure 10

The lens of the analytical eye is blind to what may be hidden or unconscious and would strongly dispute the existence of anything other than the material, visible and factual. It is only when a different eye opens, offering us another instrument, that we can see the limitations of the lens.

PAUSE POINT

Consider when and how you employ the lens in your practice as a coach.

• THE MIRROR •

The second instrument of coaching that emerges together with the opening of the appreciative eye is the mirror. The role of the mirror is to expand awareness of both the coach and client, by reflection. This is a mysterious instrument whose nature and workings extend beyond our rational comprehension. It has an enigmatic quality, so to understand how this instrument works it is useful to consider how its mystery and power have been explored in well-known stories, myths and fairy tales.

> ### PAUSE POINT
>
> **What is the value and nature of the mirror of the coach?**

MYSTERY AND MYTHS OF THE MIRROR

Alice, in *Alice in Wonderland*, was fascinated by the workings and promise of the mirror, and so she stepped through the looking glass. What she discovered was a strange new world – crazy, yet also wonderful and magical.

It is through the mirror that we can enter into a wonderland of sorts – a new world of inner experiences. This realm is feared by the rational mind because it is unknown, yet its discovery and exploration is an essential part of the journey of the coach and client.

MIRROR, MIRROR . . .

One of my earliest childhood memories was coming face to face with the talking mirror in *Snow White*. I still recall the 'mirror, mirror on the wall' scene, when the mirror appears for the first time. As a six-year-old child, I was scared to death by this mirror, largely because it had a face and could talk. Little was I to know then that I would spend my professional life cultivating such a mirror that not only had a face and could talk, but also ears, a heart, and a receptive mind, body and spirit!

THE AUTHENTIC MIRROR

The single most important aspiration of the coach is to cultivate a mirror that is authentic – one in which the client finds trust, and where, through such a mirror, the client is discovered, defined and created.

Do you search for an authentic mirror? Do you long to meet that rare person you can trust to accurately and compassionately reflect who you truly are?

My childhood experience of the mirror is a good reminder that it is not always easy to look into the mirror. Despite our longing to be discovered, we also fear the possibility.

> **The mirror of the coaching relationship has the power to reveal the clients to themselves; this is the gift, and the skill, of a masterful coach**

Fairy tales and stories that feature the mirror remind us that coaching is a voyage to facilitate self-discovery. This journey cannot be forced – the coach must check their client's commitment to enter into this journey and seek to understand the client's guiding wishes and needs. All this must be done sensitively, with pacing, while encouraging the client's prospect of self-discovery, development and learning.

EXPANDING AWARENESS AND OUR CAPACITY TO RELATE

The purpose of the mirror is to expand awareness – in both the coach and the client.

The coach expands awareness in four possible interrelated dimensions:

- self-awareness
- awareness of the other
- awareness of the influence of the collective of culture
- awareness of the larger energetic field in which we participate – the universal field.

An important relationship exists between the capacity of the coach to self-reflect and our ability to relate. One, in fact, necessitates the other. The mirror is a self-calibrated instrument. The extent to which you are able to self-reflect and self-accept is the same extent to which you can relate. What we accept in ourselves, we can unconditionally meet in others. Our capacity to self-reflect and accept therefore defines both the scope and quality of our coaching practice.

THE NATURE OF THE MIRROR

Some time ago I decided to accept an invitation to speak to a group of senior human resources professionals based in a large pharmaceutical company who wished to know how coaching actually works and what value it might offer to their staff and business. While presenting to them about the importance of the work of the coach in business, I explained the essential value of the coaching mirror. While I was explaining this, an image of Janus, a Roman god, came to mind. Janus was the god of doorways and gateways, who presided over beginnings and endings. His unique ability was that he had two heads aligned in opposite directions and could see in two different directions simultaneously.

I see the coaching mirror, like Janus's two heads, as two directional. Let me explain more fully why this is so. Have you seen in films or on television where someone who is being interviewed is unaware that there is a second presence behind the glass of a two-way mirror? Though this presence commonly goes unseen, it is ever watchful and observing. The mirror of the coach is similarly composed of these two elements: a capacity to reflect and an ever-watchful observing presence existing from somewhere behind the glass. We will revisit this aspect more fully in the next chapter.

> The living mirror is paradoxical in that it can both reflect and observe simultaneously

THE MIRROR IN PRACTICE

To demonstrate how we employ the mirror in the coaching frame, let me share a case study with you from some recent coaching work I have done.

The client, Colin, is a senior business manager in a new role with a new boss, and issues are emerging that are troubling him.

Colin: I don't know what's happening. The behaviour of my boss has been strange.

Coach: How has it been strange?

I am inviting Colin to expand his awareness through reflection.

Colin:	I have felt as though I am being watched.
Coach:	Anything more?

Are there any further deeper reflections?

Colin:	I'm making more mistakes.
Coach:	You look a little sad, Colin.

I notice sadness in Colin's eyes and decide to mirror this back. I am curious why he may be feeling this way.

Colin:	I fear failure and I'm making more mistakes than I normally make.
Coach:	I see – is there anything more?

This is a further chance to see if there are deeper reflections.

Colin:	Yes, I think I'm reaching the end of my line.
Coach:	Help me understand what that means?

I am continuing to invite an expansion of awareness.

Colin:	I have to do something – this situation has to change.
Coach:	So you've been feeling watched. Being watched is making you sad and perhaps anxious. As a result of this, you're making more mistakes. You feel you've reached the end of the line and something now needs to change.

Here I employ the help of my attentive inner observer who sits behind the glass of the mirror and reflects back to Colin the key realisations he has stated. I group them together – like grouping together key pieces of a puzzle – to give a clue to the larger emerging picture.

Colin: Yes, it's the first time that I've considered it all
            together in this way.

Coach: What part do you play in this, Colin?

*I am continuing to invite Colin to reflect and to see if he can take
responsibility for his part in this scenario.*

Colin: Mmm. I'm becoming negative and fearful,
            which may be resulting in my boss watching me
            even more.

Coach: That is insightful. Your fear of failure and
            making more mistakes is attracting the attention
            of your boss?

Colin: Yes.

Coach: What do you need? What might help you?

*The lens is now brought in to help to focus and clarify – a contrac-
tion rather than an expansion.*

Colin: I need to suggest that my boss steps back a little
            because I feel micromanaged, and that's cre-
            ating the problem. I need him to trust me a
            little more and take the pressure off myself.

Coach: How might you achieve this?

Colin: I have my performance appraisal next week and
            I'm willing to speak about this. It could be a
            win–win situation if he's willing to trust me a
            little more. I can always report on my progress,
            rather than feeling that I'm being watched.
            Maybe I can agree to let him know when I'm
            feeling micromanaged?

Coach:	Great – that's a courageous and responsible step. Is there anything more you may need to help you to take this step?
Colin:	I'll need to ask if my boss is willing for me to be honest about what I feel can be improved. If things get sticky and I need to take more time, can I come back to you to explore where to go next?
Coach:	Yes, of course. I do feel this is a positive and important step for you to take. You've both discovered and owned your own part in this. That's insightful and you've defined how you can potentially help yourself. Well done.

Here I am helping to ground the learning by mirroring how the client has taken personal responsibility for his part and is willing to act. I am reflecting how the client has demonstrated his own personal inner resourcefulness and how I sincerely appreciate the work he has done.

Colin began the session believing that the problem belonged to the new boss. As the session progressed he was able to see and take responsibility for his part in the larger sequence of events. Colin was then able to access his inner resourcefulness by realising the power and choice to consciously move this forward. The mirror of the coaching relationship was vital to this outcome. It helped Colin to obtain a wider scope, understanding and appreciation of the situation, and to own what had been hidden and previously unspoken.

THE EXPERIENCE OF BEING MIRRORED

To aid your understanding of the power and importance of the mirror in the work of the coach, let us consider how the client experiences the mirror. Recently I invited a client to describe his experience of being mirrored:

Client: I can see a self that I didn't fully understand before. I know that sounds strange, but I have been able to discover many things about myself that I would not have seen alone. Your vision and reflections have helped me to see differently. You often repeat or reflect what I have said back to me and you even reflect my mood back. I wouldn't look at myself that way on my own. It's like the back of my head – you can't see it, but coaching can help you to see it.

The mirror can sense as well as see, extending our vision – it is the essential instrument of the appreciative eye after all – so we can mirror subjective experiences such as mood, feelings or our clients' passion, for example.

THE INTERNAL AND EXTERNAL MIRROR

So far we have explored the workings of what we may call the internal mirror of the coach. A study of the mirror in coaching is not complete if we do not acknowledge the importance of a second mirror: the external mirror of nature. Let me explain and then illustrate why I believe this to be important.

> There are two types of mirror: the one we find externally in nature outside and the one that is an essential part of *our* nature

We employ the external mirror of nature when we find places where we come to rest and reflect. This process of slowing and reflecting parallels the experience in the coach–client relationship.

The places to which we are drawn in nature are personally chosen. One coaching client, Peter, who appeared in an earlier case study, has developed the habit of walking the dog on a regular basis. This represents a way of stepping out to reflect on things. He will often bring in reflections from his walks with the dog. I have a number of clients who return quite regularly to specific natural settings in order to employ the mirror, reflect and bring their experiences back into the coaching frame. Within the coaching frame these experiences can be more consciously explored and grounded, often revealing key learning for the client.

The external mirror of nature is rarely acknowledged, as little or no reference is made to the value of this mirror in the coaching literature. Similarly, if your initial reaction is to reject its use and value in coaching, before you do, please read on. I will provide illustrations taken from my own experience that support the importance of the external mirror to coaching.

If we immediately dismiss the value and importance of the external mirror, then we can miss how it may serve the growth of the client. On a very practical note, we may not be willing to free our clients to explore why they feel drawn to nature. Might we, unwittingly, limit the growth of our client by ignoring this dimension of our coaching practice?

COMBINING THE MIRRORS

Although I am separating the internal and external mirrors in order to examine them, they are, in fact, closely interrelated. When we reflect in the external mirror of nature, we remember and discover our deeper nature, the source of our passion and motivation to develop, learn and grow. The mirror of nature reminds us of our deeper authenticity and our truest and most natural self.

Nature may play an important role in helping us to rediscover our 'naturalness'

Larry is an experienced coach. In coaching supervision Larry describes how he regularly visits his favourite place in nature: a coastal walk in the UK. Wanting to understand how and why this natural setting is so important to Larry's well-being and life style, I invited him to describe what happens when he returns to this place.

Larry: When I arrive there I immediately feel free of everyday constraints that clutter my mind. I find a new and fresh perspective to things and time to reflect. This helps me to put my life and work into perspective. Time changes – it becomes quality time. I no longer rush and there seems to be more of it – time, that is. Time to reflect. It is quality 'me time' and I realise how much of my time I give away to everyone else. I somehow feel more alive and more in touch with myself. I get in touch with what is really important – what my life and work is all about. This time helps me coach. I remember why I chose to become a coach and feel as though I am on the right path and quite satisfied.

The external mirror of nature appears to provide Larry with a larger context in which the things that were previously troubling him melt away. Larry feels more in touch with his true self as a result of this experience. Nature reminds and reconnects us with our own deeper nature and helps us to recall our purpose and prospects.

Recently I coached a senior business leader of a large multinational organisation. Ian's main reason for coaching was to improve his effectiveness within a complex new role. As we worked together, Ian included his wish to process the loss of an important relationship and the feeling that something was missing from his life. Through coaching, attention was given to each and all of these areas of client interest.

As the coaching work progressed, we both noted how Ian was repeatedly bringing in strong images of nature, particularly mountains and coastlines. When we explored further, we found that these places held a deep longing – a calling to venture out into nature. Ian permitted himself the choice to take time away alone and took the initiative to have a break, choosing a particular mountainous setting. I was curious what role this might play in his coaching.

In the following session, I invited him to share his experience of this journey and what he found there that could be important to his coaching journey. This was his response:

Ian: It's the vastness (*pause*). I can see the horizon (*pause*), the sheer vastness (*pause*). Here in London it is flat and there are no mountains. It's the wonder and possibility of climbing a mountain. There's limitless opportunity.

The external mirror of nature provides Ian with a renewed sense of perspective, a chance to reflect and a sense of limitless opportunity.

Ian: It's pushing the boundaries of who I am, what you can feel and sense. At one level, my insignificance (*pause*). How the power of me can influence that vastness. It's a little mind-blowing.

With this larger perspective, Ian reflects and considers his own significance.

Ian: I would hate to have zero impact. It's about my legacy. When my bones become dust, what's important is a fulfilled life. For me, it's about relationships – staying in and building relationships. Also, what I pass on to my children and what I can influence here, through my work. There is a difference that I would love to make. This is what's important – that you have lived your life.

Note how much Ian had realised through his trip to the mountains. Ian reconnected more strongly than before with what was truly important in his life and work. He brought back into the coaching frame a new and deeper awareness of his passion and his motivation to change – an energy he can utilise in his working life.

The result of a series of trips into nature was a wish to make a difference and a need to give something back. As a result of stepping out, when he stepped back into organsational life his energy and vitality were greater. This newly discovered motivation culminated in a wish that, in some way, his work could help the developing world. Ian considered the possibility of taking a period of time out, getting directly involved in projects helping to build schools in the developing world. Ultimately a strange twist in circumstance was presented. An opportunity arose where he was able to shift the focus of his current role in the organisation to one that provided supplies of new medicines to the developing world.

Nature had reminded Ian of his deeper aspirations that he now wished to fulfil through his occupation. As our coaching concluded, Ian spoke about being more motivated, less overwhelmed and having a clearer sense of direction to his working life. I could not deny the value of the external mirror in his development through coaching.

My take-home message here is not to overlook or ignore the significance of the external mirror of wider nature to the work of the coach. In my experience, the external mirror of nature and the internal mirror of the coaching relationship combine quite naturally and fruitfully.

> ### PAUSE POINT
>
> **Do you have a place in nature? What role does nature play in your work?**

If we summarise how the mirror serves the work of the coach and combine the value of the internal and external mirrors, we discover that this instrument:

- expands our awareness, helping us to discover something more;
- helps us to conceive of a larger context that places our working lives in perspective;
- opens up the mind and heart to help us to remember the source of our innate motivation and desire to change.

Let me share how the external mirror of nature has been of value to me. Repeatedly I am drawn back to the mountains of Andalucia and village life. There I find a natural beauty that inspires and rejuvenates. The majestic landscape of mountains and sea provides a larger context. While viewing the great expanse of nature I reflect and put my own life into perspective. It was while enjoying my favourite seat (Figure 11, p.90) that I first had the idea to write this book. I returned to the same place to continue writing some of its chapters in situ.

• THE INNER COMPASS •

When the creative eye opens, two important things seem to happen: the lens and the mirror intimately combine and a further essential instrument to the work of the masterful coach emerges – the inner compass. Let us consider the importance of both of these events and how they influence and impact on your capacity to coach.

THE MIRROR AND THE LENS, IN TANDEM

With the opening of the creative eye, the limitations of both the individual lens and mirror are compensated as they combine. When the mirror is employed singly, you will recall how its limitation is an inability to structure and ground experience. The mirror greatly expands awareness, but, without a means of contracting, awareness is left open and ungrounded. The inclusion of the lens means that growing awareness can be clarified and brought into focus. In combination, the lens grounds and interprets the experience of the mirror.

Recall how the lens of the analytical eye is quick to react by processing the factual and visible. This represents only a small, limited fraction of the total energetic field. When combined with the mirror, the lens is able to process a much larger fraction and potentially the whole field of information. The inclusion of the mirror greatly increases the input of data to the

Figure 11

lens and produces a higher quality output. A representation of how the lens and mirror combine and work in tandem is shown in Figure 12, below.

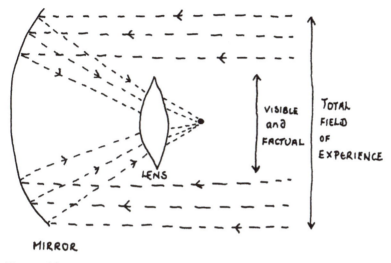

Figure 12

In the creative eye the receptivity of the mirror and its capacity to expand awareness is now grounded by the ability of the lens to contract, clarify and focus. In coaching practice, through the vision of the creative eye, the urgency of the lens to get to the answer is balanced by the curiosity of the mirror to contemplate and question.

Whereas the mirror of the appreciative eye is receptive to the possibility of the future, the lens of the analytical eye makes reference to memory and the past. In combination, the past and the future are both brought together into the prospect and possibility of the present moment. This combination offers the coach a remarkable flexibility and freedom to consciously respond.

A VARIFOCAL LENS

The lens of the creative eye becomes much more adaptable and flexible than that of the analytical eye. A recent visit to the optician gave me a better way of understanding and imagining this lens.

My own eyes appear to be changing as I age. My near and distant vision is not now totally clear. I asked the optician how he could help. He told me to try a varifocal lens. This, he explained, is a type of lens that many people now use in their spectacles that can naturally accommodate and compensate for a wide scope of possible visual limitations. This single lens has the capacity to compensate for both near and far-sightedness and so accommodates a much more unlimited vision.

I have found it useful to think of the creative eye as having a sensitive mirror and a type of varifocal lens. The lens of the creative eye can sample and process a much wider field of information, including what is sensed as well as seen.

TOWARDS THE INNER COMPASS

When combined, the mirror and lens result in the emergence of the third essential instrument of coaching – the inner compass. Somehow the dynamic flexibility of the mirror and lens to expand and contract awareness results in the emergence of a stable inner reference and guide. This is a deeper centre of identity and source that we are each invited to discover. Figure 13, opposite, is an illustration of the inner compass that shows how its discovery serves the coach.

Imagine that the inner compass highlights a point within where we are able to pivot – a place we can move from or to, allowing the coach to rebalance, reorientate and realign.

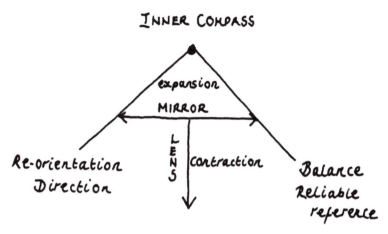

Figure 13

The inner compass is a place where we can completely come to rest and revitalise

Recognising the inner compass, we can continually realign with our source of hidden potential and power and remember and realise our desire and motivation to change.

The inner compass serves the coach in a number of important ways:

- It offers the coach a point of complete balance.
- It is a stable centre of identity where the coach can experience without being overwhelmed.
- It is a guide, providing an inner reference and a clear sense of direction.
- It reorientates and realigns us with our inner motivation to develop, learn and change.
- It deepens the attentiveness of the coach and our capacity to concentrate.

- It can sense and consciously acknowledge the larger field in which we participate and offer this new context to further the client learning.
- It locates the natural, original self as the source of our mastery.

DISCOVERING RESILIENCE

Let us consider more fully several ways in which the inner compass serves the work of the coach. This centre and inner reference gives the coach an increased sense of stability and calm. With the discovery of the compass, the inner distractions that commonly limit and distract our ability to coach are diminished and ultimately are silenced. Let me illustrate this in practice by using a case study of recent coaching work.

Mary is a physician, senior manager and a leader working in major industry. She has a very strong intellect. Her problem, and why she came to coaching, is a tendency to be over-critical, sceptical and judgemental.

We explored how Mary might apply the three eyes. We have shared and discussed the model in some detail and now Mary is considering how to put this into practice. This may seem easy – maybe too easy – but test it for yourself and explore consciously, stepping into the different viewpoints of the three eyes:

Coach:	Take your time to connect with the analytical eye. Adopt this viewpoint. Tell me, how do you experience the analytical eye?
Mary:	I know this eye well (*smile*). It's loud (*pause*).
Coach:	What's loud, Mary?
Mary:	It's really loud (*pause*), the voices in my head – telling me what I should do.
Coach:	Tell me a little more.

Mary:　　　　They judge me. In fact they're very critical
　　　　　　and harsh (*pause*). I think this is why my self-
　　　　　　esteem is quite low and maybe why I come
　　　　　　over often as critical and sceptical (*long
　　　　　　pause*).

*Mary realises how the judging and critical inner voices of the ana-
lytical eye may account for sceptical and critical persona.*

Mary:　　　　These voices keep me down and have made me
　　　　　　feel quite depressed in the past (*pause*). I hadn't
　　　　　　realised how much goes on in my head and just
　　　　　　how loud these voices are (*we smile*).

Note how the voices negatively impact her self-perception.

Coach:　　　Maybe this is the first time you've met with
　　　　　　these voices? There is a difference between real-
　　　　　　ising how loud they are and being able to
　　　　　　witness them, and being lost in their volume
　　　　　　and driven by them.

Mary:　　　　That's true.

Coach:　　　What would your experience be if you were to
　　　　　　open the appreciative eye? Would you like to
　　　　　　try?

Mary:　　　　OK.

*I step into this viewpoint within myself and recall some of the
characteristics, inviting Mary to follow suit.*

Coach:　　　Take time to step into the viewpoint of the
　　　　　　appreciative eye. Recall the characteristics of
　　　　　　this eye that we have discussed – its curiosity to
　　　　　　relate to and interest in the other, its capacity to
　　　　　　reflect – and recall how this is an eye that

operates from the inside out and places value on your experience of things. (*Long pause, I notice her smiling.*) What's happening, I'm curious?

Mary: (*Smiles*) This experience is so different from the first.

Coach: (*I smile*) How different?

Mary: No joke, it feels like sunshine (*smiling*).

Coach: What feels like sunshine?

Mary: My inner experience. It's so much lighter and quieter and the voices have gone – well almost (*pause*). That's amazing. I'm much more interested in getting to know the other person and not so self-centred. The voices have almost gone – that's amazing, isn't it?

Coach: It seems that you've found a way of stepping beyond the voices in your head to a different and quieter place?

Mary: Yes, that's true (*pause*). I think I have.

Coach: Remember this realisation, Mary. How would it be if you could work from this place?

Mary: I would be so much happier, lighter. More relaxed – less critical, less cynical

Coach: An important realisation, eh? How about your experience of the creative eye? See if you are able to step into that viewpoint. Recall how this offers a place of balance, deep reflection, and a sense of direction as you align with your desire and motivation to change. It combines each aspect of the analytical and appreciative eyes and offers a continual opportunity to be directed from the inside out (*long pause*). Are you there (*smile*)?

Mary:	Yes, I think so. It's very still and the loudness has gone completely, I think. I'm still aware of the analytical part of me, but it's more in balance now – more in check. In fact I'm balanced. That's amazing – it's so quiet here, when I'm balanced – there doesn't seem to be any voices – there's no inner nagging at all (*we smile*).
Coach:	Does it surprise you that you can find a place within of balance, calm and quiet, where you can reflect and reorientate?
Mary:	Yes. It's such a surprise. Can't quite believe it.
Coach:	That's true of part of you that can't quite believe it. Remember this place, it is there for you whenever you need it. What's it like to be there?
Mary:	Peaceful and powerful – and quite new.

PERSONAL STYLE

It was a joy to see Mary's expression change as she explored the opening of her appreciative and creative eyes. When opening the appreciative eye, her furrowed brow and serious face – a characteristic of her strong rational intellect – simply disappeared. Her face literally lit up, like sunshine.

In such moments, we realise how different reality can look by changing our inner viewpoint. Through the inner compass, we can learn how to flex our personal style. We realise the power to inwardly direct – to make choices of how we ideally wish to be from the inside out. This instrument allows us to centre and inwardly direct and master our approach.

STILLNESS AND PRESENCE

In this case study Mary arrived at the realisation of an inner point of complete balance and choice – the inner compass. This is a place of inner stillness and quiet, without distraction. If we are able to coach from this place then we are largely free from fear, doubt, cynicism and judgement. We develop an impartial and unconditional stance. Conversely, we become still, calm, responsive, confident and accepting. It is important to realise how our aspiration to become unconditional in our work is a quality that we realise from the inside out. Through the discovery of the inner compass, we deepen the quality of our relationships.

The coach is able to give their complete attention to the activity of coaching. Their ability to see, sense, relate and resolve is increased. This describes the sensitivity, responsiveness and artistry of the masterful coach, as we will explore in Chapter 6. The realisation of the inner compass increases greatly the attentiveness and concentration of the coach. If we lose sight of the inner compass when we coach, then we are unable to be still and quiet and are easily distracted by internal and external influences and events. Your ability to concentrate and coach is diminished. Without the realisation of the inner compass we are not able to give our full concentration to the activity of coaching, or place our attention on the development of our client.

THE INNER ORIENTEER AND RELIABLE GUIDE

The compass is a reliable inner guide. With the compass, the coach can navigate their way through unknown territory, confident of not getting lost or, put another way, being comfortable with not knowing either the way forward or the answer. This instrument is essential when the coach enters into the unknown and is beginning to know and understand the client more fully. Paradoxically, it is only when we surrender our certainty that we can feel the presence of the inner compass, and this realisation, in turn, gives us certainty and confidence to practise as a coach.

DEVELOPING PSYCHOLOGICAL AWARENESS

The inner compass offers the coach a place and point of deep reflection and concentration. It is through the compass that we can truly develop our psychological awareness.

From this point of stillness, the coach is able to enter deep reflection, simultaneously observing themself and their client. Using the inner compass as a stable reference point, the coach is able to identify their behaviour, inner processes and experiences from those of the client. Also, the coach can reflect upon and consider the influence and impact of the wider culture; for example, how the culture of the organisation can impact on the client and their wish to change. As the coach stills and finds this inner reference, the larger field in which the client participates becomes conscious.

> In this way, the inner compass can help the coach to realise a more universal field and context

Awareness of the inner compass provides a 3D vision that includes each of the different dimensions of awareness discussed earlier in this chapter.

PERCEIVING POTENTIAL

When you recognise your inner compass, you can stop and check in with yourself and what you are experiencing right *now*. The same applies to the client – the coach can use this reflective observation point to develop a picture of where the client is and, ideally, where they desire to be. Using the inner compass as reference, the coach can see the client's potential for development, learning and growth – a key role of the masterful coach. This is a prime position to perceive potential and provides a great opportunity for 'planting seeds'. What I mean by this is to plant seeds of an idea within the client. Seeding an idea or thought in this way does not give the client the answer, but reframes the situation by offering the potential opportunity for development.

In coaching, reaching the destiny is not the only answer. It is equally, if not more important, to be able to recognise the client's potential for growth and desire to change – the process of becoming.

THE FOUR FACULTIES OF THE INNER COMPASS

The inner compass is a place of reflection, reorientation, rest and rejuvenation. This instrument is highly receptive, in contrast to the lens of the analytical eye, which is reactive. In a way, the inner compass is a refined instrument and marks the pinnacle of the receptivity of the coach. As the coach develops awareness and increasingly employs the inner compass, four faculties emerge that are essential to masterful practice of the coach. These are intention, intuition, imagination and integrity. We will be examining the value of each of these faculties to masterful practice in Chapter 8.

• COACHING AND THE JIGSAW •

While thinking of a way to illustrate how the essential instruments of the coach combine in the vision of the creative eye, I have repeatedly been drawn to consider the jigsaw puzzle. I will use this as an analogy to demonstrate the combined value of the inner toolkit of the coach.

My sister Hazel loves jigsaws. Recently I bought her a complex one. I watched her from a distance working on her jigsaw, choosing a piece and searching for a fit. Suddenly I realised that our life's journey is not unlike the jigsaw puzzle. However, it differs from Hazel's since we don't know the picture of our completed jigsaw. In life and work we not only have to discover the different pieces of the jigsaw, but often also build it, piecing the puzzle together without knowing the whole picture. In effect, we design the jigsaw of our life in a continuum of living and we ultimately aspire to create and complete a picture of what we uniquely desire.

We discover our desire to make and complete our jigsaw from the inside out. The picture of the completed jigsaw is unique to you. What appears to be more universal is our motivation to complete the puzzle. Might we all wish to piece together our life and work in a way that makes us feel more whole, complete and satisfied? In aspiring to solve this puzzle we can make meaning of our lives and work, and develop, learn and grow.

PAUSE POINT

How does your work as a coach relate to the analogy of the jigsaw puzzle?

Our clients turn to coaching for a number of different reasons, including:

- a key piece of the puzzle is missing;
- we are not clear how, or if, our pieces fit together;
- we are feeling stuck and have lost the motivation to resolve the puzzle;
- we have little idea of where we wish to go – the picture we aspire to complete.

Coaching helps to resolve each and all of these challenges Let's explore how.

THE ESSENTIAL INSTRUMENTS AND THE JIGSAW

Through the lens of the analytical eye we often start off looking for the different pieces of the jigsaw puzzle of life, believing that each one holds the answer and solution. What the lens discovers are many different separate pieces with no apparent connection. The lens of the creative eye is vital to the study of any one piece in detail. The lens is expert in seeing how each piece is distinct and different. It brings clarity to where the client is at the moment, the exact number of different pieces and the next step he wishes to take in helping to solve the puzzle.

Through the mirror of the creative eye, the coach can help the client to bring into conscious awareness a number of different pieces of the jigsaw to consider and potentially accept and own. The client can now discover new pieces that were hidden or previously completely unknown. The capacity to reflect allows the client to look beyond any one piece of the jigsaw and to conceive of the larger whole, remembering their motivation and desire to complete the jigsaw puzzle.

The inner compass is vital in helping to piece the jigsaw puzzle together. It provides an ideal, steady and stable base from which to compile the jigsaw. It helps the client to see all the different pieces of the jigsaw and to realise how they may fit together in a way that completes the puzzle. The coach is stilled sufficiently to help the client to see the larger context that the client consciously desires. The compass can also discern those pieces of the jigsaw that belong to the client or coach – or both in some instances. Only through the creative eye and the combination of compass, mirror and lens can the puzzle be resolved and the whole picture of the puzzle be realised.

A PUZZLE WITHIN A PUZZLE

For much of our working lives, our focus is on solving the jigsaw puzzle. With the help of the coach we can discover the pieces, how they may fit together and our motivation to complete the jigsaw. However, what we realise is that completion is not the answer. Each time we realise the whole picture, the whole then appears to become a part of something larger still. Unlike the boxed jigsaw puzzle, our jigsaw does not complete and is without a solution. Might we consider the prospect that our jigsaw is but one piece of humanity's jigsaw in the making?

So what do we learn from our experience about human nature and how we develop and learn? Rather than solving the puzzle, the coach can help the client to realise that we are beings ever in the process of becoming. Self has no solution; the goal to solve and answer is not an end in itself, for there is always a new beginning. With this in mind, the need to reach an answer and to solve the problem diminishes. What becomes more meaningful is making the journey itself our destiny. The focus shifts from finding an answer to placing our attention on the current moment and activity and the chance to live more fully each step of the journey.

MASTERY AND THE JIGSAW

Instead of driving the client towards the answer, the masterful coach regards 'problems' not as something to be urgently solved, but as more sources of hidden potential with the possibility for new growth. The apparent lock becomes the client's key.

To conclude, let's explore how the three essential instruments of the coach are employed in practice – being mindful of the jigsaw. In this case study the coach's client is a senior manager who has been invited to develop her leadership skills in order to step up into a more senior role. She is a coach who is in a supervisory relationship with the author. For the sake of anonimity we will call her 'Jane'.

Jane: My client never seems to stop talking for almost all the session.

Coach: How is that for you?

While my client is speaking, I go to my inner compass and inner reference and deeply reflect, checking in with what I am experiencing in my body – my thoughts and feelings. What I realise is that I am not feeling, in fact I am quite cut off from my feelings. I am curious why this is so and what this may be telling me about my client and perhaps her client.

Jane: I have to wait patiently for a small window to open up in order to coach. It's often only for a few minutes in a whole session.

Coach: How do you feel in the session with your client?

I am very curious about how my client is feeling both now and in her sessions. So I continue to explore.

Jane: OK. I try to stay present to my client.

Coach: Imagine you are there now. Describe your experience to me.

Jane: (*Pause*) I go in and out. I sometimes feel present, but then I can lose it and feel lost. Then I feel cut off and I don't feel anything.

My client confirms my own experience – 'I feel cut off and I don't feel anything' – so how might this experience inform her work as a coach? I explore.

Coach: That's good awareness. So your experience can change as you sit with the client. Sometimes you feel present and sometimes absent. In fact, at times you don't feel anything?

I mirror back the key aspects of awareness that she has presented.

Jane: Yes. That's it.

Coach: Anything more?

Jane: I can switch off. Even though I'm sitting there, I can switch off.

Coach.   OK, so what does this tell you?

Jane: That I'm not being present enough in the coaching session?

I check in with my inner compass again – and reflect inwardly, seeking guidance and clarity of my next step . My client is seeing her experience as irrelevant to her client and that she may be doing something wrong or not quite right. I reflect and consider if this is the right time to plant a seed – something that will reframe the situ-

ation and provide a possible new context and opportunity for learning and development for my client. I decide it is the right time.

Coach:	Are you assuming that this experience and what you're sensing is all yours?
Jane:	What do you mean?
Coach:	Let me plant a seed. How might your experience inform and deepen your understanding of the client? How might your experience help to describe what your client may also be experiencing?

Seed planted – reframe made. Might her experience tell her something important about her client that may be valuable to the coaching work?

Jane:	Mmm (*pause*). That's interesting.
Coach:	Let's play with this a little. Let's see if this can foster your learning and practice. What might this tell you?

We are employing the lens to affirm, focus and ground learning.

Jane:	That my client may also be feeling in and out of relationship and quite cut off in the coaching session.

My client is working well – the seed is already growing.

Coach:	Well done. What you're sensing and experiencing may mirror what your client may be experiencing.

I am affirming and grounding the learning.

Jane:	That helps me to understand so much more (*pause*). I always feel in my head when I'm with this client and maybe that's where my client is?

Coach: Good. How does this new awareness inform your work with the client?

Can this new awareness inform her practice? We are employing the lens to focus and clarify.

Jane: When I feel cut off, I could ask how she is feeling?

Coach: How might that serve?

Jane: It gives the client a chance and opportunity to own and say how she may be feeling. She may also be able to talk about being stuck or cut off. We would be relating a little more – things would be more real, more authentic – if she were able to do that. This may be limiting how she relates and her performance.

I check in with my compass for direction and decide to help to ground the learning while also mirroring the paradox of her client – how activity may hide a sense of feeling stuck and cut off. I sincerely acknowledge her willingness to explore working in this way.

Coach: Good. It's interesting, isn't it? Our clients may be exceptionally busy and fill the coaching space with words, but beneath a very active intellect they might be feeling quite stuck. Possibly cut off from their feelings and out of relationship with themselves. This mirrors what you were experiencing in this session. The question is: how might this inform your work with the client?

Jane: I think I've got it. I'll practise working with this.

Coach: Great. Bring your learning back into supervision.

This case study illustrates the use of the three essential instruments and shows how the coach can work to discern unconscious processes. Such awareness and learning can deepen the practice of the coach while fostering the client's development and growth.

We have explored three essential instruments of the coach – the lens, the mirror and the compass, and how these can combine through the creative eye to allow the coach the opportunity to practise more masterfully. Through the coaching relationship we can discover, affirm and create who we are. In realising that our jigsaw is never complete, we give ourselves the permission to look behind and to recognise our true, genuine and most natural self rather than seek the answer. This is the secret to our mastery, which we will explore more fully in Chapter 6.

C h a p t e r   F i v e

SUPER-VISION

• • •

Here we will look at what *super*-vision is, its importance to the continuing development of the coach and how this practice helps to bring an individual, relational, cultural and universal awareness to your coaching.

• • •

When a client places trust in the coaching relationship, the eyes and vision of the coach can essentially be shared. As we have already explored, the intention of the coach is always to expand awareness and vision – to cultivate *super*-vision. In extending the field of vision, the coach provides the same prospect and possibility for the client.

• WHAT IS SUPERVISION? •

Linguistically, supervision can be a confusing word. A supervisor may at one level be seen as someone who knows best and takes charge of a supervisee. Supervision is also a modern professional practice, operating in multiple professions, whose single goal is to help the practitioner to step back and reflect on their practice in order to return with greater awareness and considered and informed interventions that may best serve their clients. This provides the practitioner with an opportunity to question: What am I learning? What might I be missing? How can I serve my client better? Where can I grow?

• COACHING THE COACH •

The supervisory relationship is a mirror of that of the coach and client. In supervision, the coach steps into the role of the client to consider how the client may be better served through the coaching relationship. In essence the supervisor is the coach of the coach, and the resulting practice is coaching supervision. As the coach is able to help the client to extend their vision, the coach requires a further coach to continue the expansion of their own.

• APPRENTICESHIP •

Supervision is an apprenticeship where the coach literally learns through practice. It may be somewhat of a revelation to realise that in the journey of discovering mastery the coach is invited repeatedly to step into the role of the client and to develop and refine practice.

The aspiration to become an exceptional coach mirrors an openness to be coached – one necessitates the other

The coach–supervisor relationship mirrors that of the coach–client, and both share the goal of helping the clients in question – to extend how they see, sense, relate and resolve.

• CHOOSING A SUPERVISOR •

Since this is an essential relationship to your work and developing practice, your choice of supervisor is very important. Choose carefully. Supervision can be a challenging and supportive environment of continual exploration and learning. You therefore need to choose someone you respect and with whom you can develop a very trusting relationship. I stress the importance of this choice because this is your main learning environment and where you can be supported in how to extend your practice.

PRACTICALITIES

There are no set guidelines for supervision. The time dedicated to supervision will depend on the size of your coaching practice. Normally the coaches I supervise dedicate a minimum of three hours per month to supervision. I also personally appreciate being able to make contact with my supervisor if and when something urgent arises. A dedicated and agreed time slot, and the possibility of access to your supervisor in between times if and when necessary, is the ideal situation.

INDIVIDUAL OR GROUP

You can choose individual or group supervision, or both. Obviously individual supervision involves you working one to one with a supervisor, while in the group setting several coaches work together with a single supervisor. The choice depends on you and the stage of your journey and practice. Supervision helps to build your confidence to practise and, for the new coach, one to one may initially be preferable. In group supervision, the learning experience amplifies and may be of particular value to the more experienced coach. Both are important options at all times, irrespective of your level of experience.

• THE GOAL OF SUPERVISION •

Supervision is a relationship through which the coach can continue to learn and extend their practice: as vision expands, so does your capacity to relate and help to resolve. Once more supervision mirrors coaching practice in its multidimensional approach, developing different dimensions of awareness. These include:

Self-awareness – how you experience things

- Understanding your own psychological process and inner experiences.

Relational awareness – your awareness of others

- Your ability to sense where others may be.
- Your capacity to discern your psychological process from those of your clients.
- Understanding your client's psychological process and needs relative to your own.
- Your ability to empathically relate.

Cultural awareness

- How the collective experience of culture can influence and impact on your client.

Universal awareness

- Becoming aware of the larger energy field in which we participate as a context to make meaning that parallels the realisation of original self.

Although we can differentiate our field and scope of awareness in this way, these dimensions are intimately associated in practice.

• SUPERVISION IN PRACTICE •

Rather than describing supervision from the outside looking in, let me share another recent example of coaching supervision to illustrate its value and application, mindful of the different levels of awareness that allow the coach to see, sense and relate.

Cheryl is a practising coach of two years. Here is an extract from our conversation in supervision. Her client, Ivan, is a senior businessman who has entered coaching for the first time and is exploring the prospect of stepping up to the next level of leadership. He has entered into a coaching relationship to help him to achieve this prospect.

First I check in with my client to see how she is today and if there are any major needs.

Supervisor:	So how are you? Check in with me.
Cheryl:	(*Pause*) Doing well, I think. My practice is growing slowly (*pause*). I'm enjoying coaching but sometimes I feel a little out of my depth.
Supervisor:	Tell me more.
Cheryl:	I am working with a senior client – a successful businessman – and something is getting in the

	way of the work. I'm not sure what. I just feel uncomfortable, somehow.
Supervisor:	Can you share a scene from your work when you feel something is getting in the way?
Cheryl:	Sure (*pause*). It's when I meet with him that it begins. I walk into the office and say 'Hello' to Ivan and immediately I begin to feel anxious. It takes me a good while before I can settle into the coaching.
Supervisor:	Share a little more? Help me to understand.
Cheryl:	Well, when I meet Ivan I suddenly become anxious and quite nervous. I lose my professional edge and become a bit girly.
Supervisor:	What's going on inside?
Cheryl:	I'm anxious and feel scared – off centre – and it's hard for me to settle for some time. It takes me a while to feel as though I'm able to coach. Something gets in the way.
Supervisor:	So you walk in, feel anxious and scared and something gets in the way of your ability to coach. Do you feel you lose something?
Cheryl:	Yes (*pause*), my power to coach.
Supervisor:	That's good awareness. Tell me something of your inner conversation with yourself.
Cheryl:	(*Smiles, long pause*) The voice in my head says that Ivan is a powerful businessman and I'm just a little coach. It says judgementally and quite cynically 'What makes you think that you can help?' I crumble a little and become shy and awkward – somehow younger.

I am pleased that Cheryl is willing to be authentic about her own psychological process here.

Supervisor: What do you realise in speaking this?

Cheryl: I've got it wrong somehow.

Note how Cheryl has immediately personalised this awareness, believing that she has done something wrong. Listening to the judging voice, she has become self-judging. I want to see if Cheryl can look beyond the analytical eye to see how this awareness may also be relevant to her coaching practice

Supervisor: No Cheryl, you haven't. There's nothing wrong. You're being asked or invited to deepen your awareness in order to coach more successfully in this situation. How can you work with this? What might you learn from this?

Cheryl: I hadn't realised how loud this voice was in my head when I meet with Ivan – the judging voice, I can't stop it and it takes my power away.

I want to explore if Cheryl can see if this voice of judgement may in some way serve her so that she can learn to see beyond its judgement. Is there a place of acceptance of this voice?

Supervisor: OK, so this voice limits you. But also how does this voice serve you?

Cheryl: Mm (*pause*). I'm not sure. I didn't consider that it might.

Supervisor: Take your time.

Cheryl: (*Pause*) Well, strangely it reminds me of my commitment to coach – why I am a coach.

Supervisor: Say more?

Cheryl:	Well, in saying to me 'What makes you think that you can help?' I do become anxious, but what it also makes me do now is to look a bit deeper into the reason why I coach.
Supervisor:	Why do you coach?
Cheryl:	I'm deeply interested in human nature and what makes us tick – how we get stuck and need someone else to help us realign and grow. That's why I coach. I care deeply about this process and the people – my clients. I really do.

I notice a shift in Cheryl's energy in line with this new personal awareness – more powerful and agile, no longer stuck – and I wonder if Cheryl can ground the learning from this experience.

Supervisor:	How are you feeling now?
Cheryl:	Strong, centred and much clearer – empowered.
Supervisor:	Notice how you have moved from feeling disempowered to being empowered when you remember why you coach. What are you learning from this with regards to your work with Ivan?
Cheryl:	(*Pause*) If I can remember why I coach, then I don't lose my power.
Supervisor:	Good. How will you remember?

I am again impressed by Cheryl's learning and want her to explore how she can make this relevant to her practice.

| Cheryl: | (*Pause*) I'll carry something in my pocket – a talisman. Something I can hold just to help me remember why I'm there. |

Supervisor:	How creative (*we smile*). Do you feel this has helped your own process in relation to Ivan?
Cheryl:	Yes. I have made something conscious that was getting in the way before. I didn't know why, now I do. Yes it has.

I realise that there is a larger relational awareness and context that may bring more learning for Cheryl and I decide to explore.

Supervisor:	Can we work with this a little further to look at your coaching work with Ivan?
Cheryl:	Yes.
Supervisor:	How might what you are learning speak to the work with Ivan?
Cheryl:	I'm not sure.
Supervisor:	Take your time.
Cheryl:	There's something missing, if I'm honest. It's hard going – the coaching feels like hard work.
Supervisor:	What do you mean by hard going?
Cheryl:	Well, I seem to do most of the work in the coaching relationship.
Supervisor:	Anything more?
Cheryl:	I'm not sure we're getting anywhere fast.
Supervisor:	Well done, Cheryl. I have a strong hunch you're right.

My hunch is that Ivan may not be fully engaged in the coaching relationship.

Cheryl:	Really?
Supervisor:	Yes. Let's summarise. You walk in – you immediately feel 'What makes you think that you can help?': something seems to be missing

	from the coaching and you experience not getting anywhere fast. What might be missing?
Cheryl:	In Ivan?
Supervisor:	How might your experience – what you feel – say something about the coaching relationship?
Cheryl:	I'm not quite getting it yet.
Supervisor:	OK. What is essential to a successful coaching relationship?
Cheryl:	Trust. The trust is missing.
Supervisor:	How do you foster trust?
Cheryl:	Setting the coaching frame in the first place.
Supervisor:	Right. Can you piece it together?
Cheryl:	(*Long pause*) Got it! Ivan might not be committed to the coaching relationship.
Supervisor:	Spot on. How do you know?
Cheryl:	My immediate feeling of 'What makes you feel that you can help?' – might he also be feeling that?
Supervisor:	Well done. So let's reflect together. You walk in and feel this way. You find it difficult to settle into coaching and something feels missing – his commitment maybe? How strong is the coaching frame? Where might you go from here?
Cheryl:	Wow. You know I've had a hunch with Ivan that the coaching has not been somehow working. I need to revisit our contract and be willing to check his commitment to the work.
Supervisor:	Good. How might that serve?
Cheryl:	(*Pause*) Maybe there is a reason why he is not committed to the work? That's what is missing.
Supervisor:	Very good. What intervention might you make to check this out?

I am continuing to ground her learning to make it relevant to her practice.

Cheryl:	I'll speak to him about his commitment and how the coaching is progressing or not, and what we might need to put in place or decide to do.
Supervisor:	When will you commit to do this, Cheryl?
Cheryl:	Next session – this month.
Supervisor:	Good. Well done – you have an important intervention and learning to check out that has emerged today.

At our next session, Cheryl and I review progress.

Cheryl:	I want to talk about Ivan after our last session.
Supervisor:	Tell me?
Cheryl:	Well, I felt differently walking in – I took my talisman in my pocket and felt more conscious about what was happening. I remembered my reason for being there. It was easier.
Supervisor:	Well done – so your strategy worked?
Cheryl:	Yes, I did remember why I was there. It was much easier for me to stay present. When I started the coaching session I realised that I seemed to be doing all the work somehow. So remembering the last supervision, I said, 'There's something I want to explore with you Ivan – I'm wondering how committed you are to the coaching work. On a scale of 1 to 10, may I ask you honestly how committed are you to our work?'

He was surprised by the question. His answer was about 5. I invited him to be very open with me and let me know what was happening and why his commitment was only 5. He said that he was participating in the coaching because his boss felt it was important, but he wasn't fully engaged. He actually mellowed after speaking this and the conversation felt very real. I told him that the choice was entirely his and said we could end if he wished. But he wanted to continue. I said to Ivan, 'This is your time. What do you really want to gain from this?' He told me that he was lacking commitment to his work at the moment and felt a little lost. I asked if he would like to explore this and his response was clearly yes. We had a new context to our work, one to which he was visibly much more committed.

Supervisor: Excellent.

Cheryl: Look what came out of the last supervision session! It seems that the work is all around commitment and engagement.

Supervisor: Is that a surprise?

Cheryl: In some way yes, but very useful.

Supervisor: So what are you learning from this?

Cheryl: That my experience – what I feel – matters, and not to over-personalise it or make it wrong. It may be valuable to what's happening in the coaching relationship. I can use it more creatively – through supervision – here.

I am delighted with Cheryl's learning and relational awareness.

Supervisor: Well done. Because you helped Ivan to own his lack of commitment, has he more fully committed to the coaching do you think?

Cheryl: Yes.

I have been musing whether Ivan's lack of commitment is in relation to his boss or something wider, so I decide to explore.

Supervisor: If you were to step into Ivan's shoes for the moment, what do you think he is actually telling you about his commitment?

Cheryl: (*Pause*) Because his boss wanted him to have a coach this has affected his commitment to the coaching – rather than engage he has disengaged. With hindsight I should have checked the frame better when we began.

Supervisor: Good. Carry on. What might be happening?

Cheryl: Ivan is also not committed to his job.

Supervisor: Might there be a cultural element to this also, do you know?

Cheryl: That's interesting. He did talk about culture in our last session – a blame culture. That it was dangerous to fully engage for fear of being too visible and blamed.

Supervisor: Remind me of the context for coaching.

Cheryl: To see if Ivan could step up to the next level of leadership and management.

Supervisor: So what are you seeing?

Cheryl: That the culture may also be negatively impacting the intention of the coaching.

Supervisor: How can you work with this awareness?

Cheryl: I need Ivan to help me to understand the impact of the culture more, and how this might affect the goal of the coaching work – his stepping up to a more visible role

I am aware over the two sessions how Cheryl has worked with personal, relational and cultural awareness and wish to acknowledge this and mirror how all three dimensions are important within supervision.

Supervisor: Good. Do you see how you have been working with your personal, relational and cultural awareness in these sessions?

Cheryl: Yes, and they all interrelate.

Supervision: Note your widening field of vision. It's good awareness, Cheryl.

In this case study three of the four dimensions of awareness are explored – namely self, relational and cultural awareness. Note how Cheryl learns how her own feelings can, in parallel, indicate something important about the client's experience. In making her feelings fully conscious, Cheryl creates the opportunity to explore how this experience may help her to learn about her client and further inform her future coaching interventions. A cultural dimension is also recognised – how the organisational field can impact on the behaviour of the individual client. Note how the key to change is in making both these dimensions conscious. Once consciously owned, the client is somehow freed from their grip. A space is created for reflection and a deeper consideration of their relevance and meaning.

ANOTHER SUPERVISORY EXAMPLE

Let me also share a recent example where a more universal dimension of awareness comes into play.

Derek has been an experienced coach for ten years. He is working with a client Sheila, who has been feeling very stuck in her work. Sheila is a senior human resources director and has entered into a coaching relationship to find a way of moving forward.

Derek:	I experienced something strange and wonderful in one of my coaching sessions.
Supervisor:	Sounds intriguing.
Derek:	Yes it is. Let me set the scene. I've been working with Sheila who has been feeling stuck. The coaching work has been going well – we have a good open and trusting relationship. I have really been able to help her to explore her feeling stuck.
Supervisor:	What was the turning point?
Derek:	(*Pause*) Er, Sheila had got in touch with feeling really lost and had got upset and had actually shed a few tears and didn't know the way forward. I affirmed to Sheila that the answer was inside her and not me. I expressed strongly that I truly believed that she knew deep down what she needed and what needed to happen to move things forward. The penny seemed to drop – she suddenly realised that she had been looking to everyone else to find the answer – everyone other than herself.
Supervisor:	What was your experience?

Derek:	She suddenly stopped and realised that she had the answer and that this was around being able to include more of what she most enjoyed in her life and work. She grew calm and quiet and smiled. Sheila then went on to talk about the freedom of playing on the beach as a child. I asked if she was experiencing that freedom now, and she said yes. It was strange – we seemed very deeply connected although we didn't say very much. Sheila had found something within and the time together just seemed to somehow disappear.
Supervisor:	What had she found?
Derek:	A new self-belief. She realised that she was in charge of her own life – you know – only she could navigate her boat, sort of thing. No one else, and it was a revelation. Time passed in a second and it was almost the end of the session before I knew it. Nothing was rushed, it was just right somehow. We were very closely connected even though we said little. There was stillness and long periods of quiet where we didn't feel we needed to speak.
Supervisor:	How do you make sense of this experience?
Derek:	Sheila remembered something vital and it changed things. She remembered who she was – who she is – she got in touch with her real self somehow. It was like nothing else was needed really. I just witnessed her and mirrored her energy and joy. Everything seemed to move and fit in that instant.

Supervisor:	What was your experience?
Derek:	I marvelled at this revelation and felt so calm and at peace. It made me realise what this work is about – truly about. Helping people to be themselves within their chosen occupation. I did ask Sheila what had changed at the end of the session and she said everything and nothing, and smiled. I wanted to understand and help her to ground this more fully, so I asked her something like 'What are you taking from this?' Her response was: 'I need to make changes for myself and I've been waiting for someone else to make it better, but I can only do this for myself.' It was an important realisation.
Supervisor:	Were you changed by this experience?
Derek:	Yes. I felt affirmed – very real and authentic in my work.
Supervisor:	(*Smiling*) You were sharing the same parallel experience as Sheila.
Derek:	Wow, yes, maybe.

Here, the client of the coach in supervision describes the experience of remembering original self and develops a more universal awareness, recognising a larger context in which the meaning of things profoundly change. Something suddenly appears to fit into place: a realisation and order from amidst disorder. Time seems to take a different measure, together with an experience of being in flow and a joy and deep sense of authenticity and wholeness. Such characteristic experiences will often mark a major shift in a client's awareness and self-identity. The masterful coach is comfortable to facilitate, mirror and help to ground such experiences in coaching and supervision.

• SUMMARY •

Mirroring the coach and their client, the supervisory relationship is based on trust. It is one where the supervisor is consciously seeking to guide the development and growth of the coach. Just as the coach seeks to help their client to expand their vision and awareness, so the supervisor similarly guides the coach to take another progressive step along this journey of deepening awareness and the ability to more sensitively relate. Through supervision we learn to trust our senses to guide us in what may be unspoken within the coaching relationship and in supervision. In building this trust our confidence to practise grows.

It is the work of both the supervisor and the coach to help to transform that which is unconscious or partially conscious into full awareness, allowing vision to expand and sensitivity to deepen. We discover new choices in making the unconscious conscious, transforming reaction into response. We learn to see how we can confine ourselves and our understanding of the other. In taking a personal and isolated view of our experiences, we forget the wider field of which our experience is a part.

Chapter Six

DISCOVERING THE MASTERFUL COACH

• • •

Here we explore three different self-identities – the ego, inner observer and original self, representing the viewpoints of the analytical, appreciative and creative eyes respectively. You will discover how, in adopting the inner observer, you awaken an interior rather than an exterior view of reality, question rather than answer and expand awareness, choice and your capacity to relate. As you learn to still, concentration increases and inner distractions minimise, allowing you to place your attention purely on the client and the activity of coaching. This leads to the discovery of a deeper centre of identity (original self) that is the source of awareness and power of the masterful coach.

• • •

As we learn to expand our vision, we meet with different identities that comprise our understanding and concept of self. In becoming these different selves we alter our capacity to coach, since they inform the way we see, sense, relate and resolve. To coach others, we need primarily to discover the identity of the inner coach. Our capacity to coach and its mastery is discovered from the inside out. The masterful coach is the person you are invited to be and become. Let's explore this journey of being or becoming a masterful coach by examining the nature of these different coaching selves and how they each influence our coaching practice.

• THE FIRST SELF – THE EGO •

When we adopt the position of a detached observer and look at things from the outside in, we discover the ego. This provides us with a sense of security and containment, affirming our identity and rightness. However, in selecting the good from the bad, the ego subdivides the self. A partial self is created and we are compartmentalised, with a limited view of reality. Yet the ego is without doubt that its vision and knowledge is absolute. The consequence of striving for security and seeing things objectively is that we literally turn a blind eye to the interior world of subjective experience. We devalue our deeper emotions, values and aspirations and instead focus on what is factual, visible and can be rationally known.

We have already explored how the eye of the ego – the analytical eye – is driven to rationalise and answer, rather than to question and relate. These distinctive character traits of ego limit the possibility of coaching. In order to develop our capacity to coach and to step towards becoming a masterful coach, we have to somehow recognise that the vision of the ego is limited and we must learn how to

PAUSE POINT

How well do you know your egoistic self? What does it look like? How does it limit and serve your coaching practice?

(Do not be surprised if these questions seem challenging. We commonly do not question our viewpoint or how well we see things. We assume that the view from the ego is all there is.)

extend our way of seeing. Do not underestimate the size of this challenge. Convincing an eye that is sure of its knowledge and certain of its rightness that it has limitation and blindness is one of the key challenges that we and humanity face. Much of our conflict and division arises from the certainty and conviction of the analytical eye.

• THE EMERGENCE OF THE INNER OBSERVER •

Discovering the inner observer involves the emergence of a new identity and aspect of the self, distinct from that of the ego. When coaching, I am often aware that while noticing my client, I am also able to notice myself, noticing my client. Here I have stepped into the position of the inner observer and become a witness. When we see through the eyes of the inner observer – the appreciative eye – new and different perspectives become available. When I coach from this position, I can clearly see both myself and my client, and observe how we are relating. Through the inner observer, the coach can now step beyond an exterior view to enter the interior world of subjective experience and learn how to sense. This explains the dualistic characteristics of the Janus-like two-way mirror described in Chapter 4 – the capacity to observe and reflect simultaneously.

OBSERVING FROM BEHIND THE GLASS

I imagine the inner observer being behind the glass of our two-way living mirror. When we acknowledge this presence, we once more recognise our ability to witness, reflect and relate. Have you ever looked closely at a mirror to see how it is made? You will discover that there is a film of quicksilver intimately attached to the glass that gives the mirror its ability to reflect. The poem below alludes to the enigmatic nature and value of the inner observer to the work of the coach.

QUICKSILVER

imperceptibly close
a breath away
your tide calls
in the ebb and flow
i yearn to be seen
my temptation to hide

like sunlight on water
do you bathe in quicksilver
vibrant and real
yet quite untouchable
just beyond the visible
yet seeing all

what a selfless gift
to offer your eyes
that in discovering you
i too

can discover

my true

self

(taken from *Just Beyond the Visible: The Art of Being and Becoming*)

Through the discovery of the inner observer, the coach is inwardly taught how to become a more patient, attentive and reflective witness, and, in turn, is able to relate empathetically. This realisation gives value and place to the importance of our interior world of experience in the process of development and learning.

PAUSE POINT

What is your experience of the inner observer when you coach? How does adopting this position serve and limit your practice?

SEEING BLINDNESS

One of the important gifts the inner observer gives to the coach is that we awaken to our blindness. In stepping into a place where we can simply witness, we are able, for the first time, to step back from and see our previous attachment and where we have been identified. When I realise the inner observer, I am no longer driven to rationalise and answer; instead I can slow down and reflect; my thinking becomes more open and receptive. Whereas, before, I would rationalise, now I can observe and watch my thoughts without a need to process them. The coach who works from the position of the inner observer is less distracted and becomes much more able to focus on the activity of coaching. In being able to see and accept one's limitation, a further window is opened to a more expanded and unlimited vision. This is a very important paradox that we need to carefully consider: in accepting limitation we are able to glimpse more of the unlimited.

Stepping beyond the urgency to solve problems, the coach experiences a new sense of inner spaciousness. This is the experience of being able to let go, or what I call the ability to not know. We no longer feel compelled to answer and this frees the coach within us to question. The inner observer offers a deeper concentration and curiosity to the work of the coach and the capacity to contemplate. These are some of the characteristics of the masterful coach.

THE INNER OBSERVER IN PRACTICE

Often when I start a coaching session I imagine that I am moving my attention from my head to my body. I link this conscious shift to my breathing, and I take three long, slow breaths. With each in-breath, I consciously move my attention downwards towards my heart, and with each out-breath let my attention expand into my body. While I am very aware of consciously opening and seeking to expand my awareness and sensitivity, this probably goes completely unnoticed by my client.

Here, I am consciously shifting my awareness to a position where I can observe, sense and listen more intently – to the inner observer. My motivation in making this conscious shift is to more fully understand the needs and desires of my client. I become aware of my inner world, I am deeply curious of what I am feeling and sensing, and I wonder what my client may be experiencing. In my self-reflections I am curious how my own experience might relate to that of my client. I consciously expand my awareness while considering each of these different perspectives of the coaching relationship.

In being willing to consciously expand my awareness beyond the confines of self to better sense, appreciate, understand and care for another, I am guided in how to realise empathy. The inner observer, in essence, teaches the coach how to relate, helping the coach to appreciate and understand the client.

INSIDE OUT

Through the eye of the inner observer – the appreciative eye – the coach can enter into a world of subjective experience. We begin to sense rather than see. To make this shift it is necessary that we invert our perception of reality. We are invited to learn how to turn our perceptions inside out.

In the coaching relationship I often experience my clients arriving at a crossroads or a turning point. Figure 14, p.134, captures the dilemma of the turning point for me.

Like the snail in the snapshot, facing the turning point is not easy and appears to have no rational solution. When you coach, listen carefully to how your clients describe this experience. Their old way of doing things no longer seems to satisfy, but there is no way forward, and no way back. Where do we go from here? An essential aspect of the work of the coach is to help clients to face and negotiate these crossroads, and use this 'problem' as an opportunity to expand their vision by turning their perception of reality inside out, towards the subjective.

When the turning point resolves, I commonly experience a sense of release in the coaching relationship. This often parallels a recon-nection with the client's desire to change – a re-engagement and renewed sense of responsibility and commitment to change. When driving forward no longer works, it is then that we are invited to learn how to relax, turn inward and experience a greater sense of

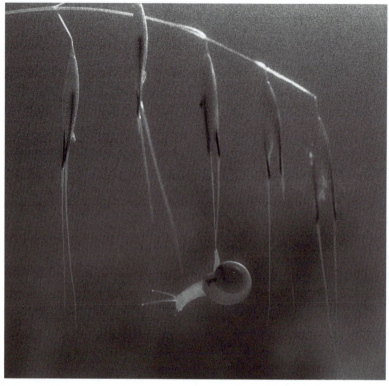

Figure 14

inner space and stillness. Becoming still parallels the process of being able to let go. Not needing to know replaces the urgency to answer. As the coach consciously adopts the position of the inner observer, we model for the client the prospect and possibility of being able to open one's mind and heart. Thinking becomes more receptive and the quality of the coaching relationship deepens.

PACE AND SPACE

Time and again when I coach I realise how the analytical eye, in its preoccupation with needing to work and be somewhere else, ignores how truly busy we are. Clients who operate from the position of the ego and analytical eye often find the concept of a life–work balance out of reach. In my experience, such clients are often unaware of the extent of their own tiredness and exhaustion. It is only when the coach discovers the inner observer that such a reflective space can be shared through the coach–client relationship. It is here that clients can begin to explore a more extended vision, and feelings of tiredness can be owned. The capacity to manage pace and create space is another important characteristic of the masterful coach.

• THE SECOND SELF – ORIGINAL SELF •

In Chapter 2 we explored the concept of two selves. The first self is a partial self that the ego appears to create. It is the mask through which we meet the world and it is a self that is deemed to be acceptable, often meeting the expectations and judgement of others who have most influenced our lives. The ego can give us a strong sense of identity and yet the consequence is that we can spend much of our lives meeting other people's expectations, rather than permitting ourselves the things we most enjoy and love.

Through the emergence of the inner observer, we conceive of a second self – 'the self in potential'. This is the whole of which you are – the original self. Through the position of the inner observer, life develops directionality. Our partial self aspires to become more whole – the first self seeks to finds its place and fit within the whole of the second self. In essence, the inner observer facilitates and guides this process.

Whereas the ego is concerned with multiplicity and the original self with unity, the inner observer makes us aware of the dynamic relationship between our partiality and wholeness. This highlights an essential aspect of the work of the coach, which is to help to make conscious the potentiality and motivation of the client to develop and change.

In studying the process of how we develop and grow, the coach comes to realise the importance of our partial wholeness. As we accept this as an aspect of our deeper and truest nature, the coach learns to see the importance of the paradoxical nature of reality and realises that we are in fact human beings ever in the process of becoming.

As we move close to realising the original self, the coach experiences a deepening attentiveness and a capacity to still and stop. The coach can relax and simply notice everything. Inner distractions become calmed and quietened. The judging, critical and sometimes cynical voices that resound within our heads that instruct us in what we must or should do, quieten and are ultimately silenced. We can place our attention purely upon the activity in hand – coaching – without distraction or condition. If the coach can make conscious the source of our motivation to change, then the realisation of the original self becomes an expression of our innate vitality to change – we experience being in flow. Change then becomes spontaneous and inspired.

PAUSE POINT

How might you experience 'stilling' in practice? How does this experience serve and inform your work?

STILLING AND STOPPING

Let me illustrate the importance of this process of stilling, and ultimately stopping, to the work of the coach by sharing an analogy that I use while coaching.

STILLED LIFE

When I walk in nature with my camera I will suddenly notice something that draws my attention and catches my eye. My pace slows and I stop. I begin to look more closely and observe. I am always curious about why I am drawn to and stilled by certain subjects. I position my camera, focus and take the snapshot.

What is truly a marvel is how, through the medium of photography, we can capture a particular moment on film for posterity. Such moments can be seen in detail by examining the snapshot. What I realise when I do study these instances of 'stilled life' is that I am able to see so much more in the snapshot than I noticed in that same moment in reality. When we are busy it seems we miss much of present reality. The moment is passed and our view of it is fleeting. The coach learns how to still and stop in order to help the client to become more aware of current reality and appreciate the fuller picture and true scope of the present moment.

STILLING IN PRACTICE

When you coach, watch for the moments when things begin to still and the client begins to pause and reflect. In these moments I often imagine that I am taking a snapshot. I then muse over what I might discover if I were to study the snapshot in detail – what might I have overlooked or missed in this passing moment? As the pace slows, the capacity to reflect extends, awareness is expanded and we mysteriously see more of present reality than we did before.

The capacity to create space and the ability to still and stop is once more a vital marker of the emergence of the inner compass and is another characteristic of the masterful coach. We discover an inner balance or pivot point to which we can return again and again in our practice. This is a point at which we can consciously re-orientate and realign ourselves with our motivation to change.

When we centre and still, we are free to choose and act

• REMEMBERING OUR ORIGINAL CIRCUITRY •

As we meet with the different self-identities explored in this chapter, the authenticity of the coach continues to deepen. We become more real and natural. Previous divisions that were confining now disappear and dissolve and, together with a feeling of being more complete and whole, we experience being in flow.

One way of considering the experience of being in flow is that we, in realising the original self, complete a long forgotten yet vital circuit. Commonly this deeper circuit is unavailable to us, something has 'tripped' – the circuit is broken. Our motivation, desire and will to change is lost to us, yet we somehow know it is there and long to find it. We search for what will complete this original circuitry and provide access to our hidden potential. It is only when we realise the paradox of our ways that we unravel this dilemma. Although we are driven to search for the answer – to find our circuit maker – the need to search and our striving to find is in fact the circuit breaker.

It is important for us to realise, and deeply appreciate, that we and our clients may search endlessly for the answer only to discover that the answer is not to search.

The opportunity then exists for the client, through the coaching relationship, to begin to look and turn inwards, to value the personal experience, and continue the journey to discover the inner observer and, ultimately, original self.

• PARADOX: THE CIRCUIT MAKER •

In my experience, when clients realise their paradoxical nature, somehow they reconnect with and remember an inner source of power and choice.

> Rather than experience division, difference and conflict, we can learn to see and embrace the natural contradiction of things

Paradox illustrates a secret deeper relationship that can exist between apparently contradictory elements. Paradox is a portal to a deeper appreciation of reality and a knowledge that guides us close to remembering our original self.

PARADOX IN PRACTICE

Let me share an example of a recent case study where the naming of paradox shifted the client from feeling stuck to discover a much clearer way forward. Adam has a very senior role with major complex responsibilities. When he checked in he was feeling confined and wrongly judged by his new boss, who had given him a poor assessment despite all his very hard work and conscientiousness. Adam is talking about his boss:

Adam: She is quite demanding; she needs a lot of information – she really is needy. It's hard work giving her everything she wants and I don't get

thanked for it. I just get picked up on the one
mistake I've made. My work is scrutinised.

I note that Adam is referring to his boss, Margaret, as 'she'. I
wonder if Adam realises how devaluing this sounds. It makes me
curious about how Adam truly feels about his boss.

Coach:	How do you feel about your boss?
Adam:	She's hard going.
Coach:	How do you feel? Do you respect Margaret?
Adam:	(*Pause*) No, I don't. She's not working in a way that I can respect.
Coach:	Adam, since you've been talking about Margaret, you have on every occasion referred to her as 'she'.
Adam:	Sorry!

Adam is a little shocked and did not realise this.

Coach:	I'm not judging you, Adam, just observing. Let's look at what is covertly being said. If I have picked up on how you are referring to your boss as 'she', then it's likely that others may have too. What if your boss has picked this up? If you were your boss and picked this information up, how would you feel?
Adam:	(*Pause*) Probably judged and disrespected. I would keep a tight rein and may not trust.
Coach:	Do you recognise this behaviour?
Adam:	Yes, quite accurately.
Coach:	Let's name the paradox here. You are feeling judged and devalued, almost disrespected for the hard work that you are doing.
Adam:	Yes.

Coach:	But you are also devaluing, disrespecting and judging Margaret.
Adam:	Mmm (*pause*), that's true and I hadn't realised.
Coach:	Where do we go from here?
Adam:	(*Pause*) I want to try to work on this relationship and see if I can move the trust forward.

In naming the paradox, Adam can see his part in the whole dynamic and he becomes clearer on how he would like to respond and move things forward.

Coach:	Are you willing to do that?
Adam:	Yes.
Coach:	Good. Let's do it then.

Adam explored looking at the situation appreciatively, rather than seeing it through an analytical and judging eye – paradoxically with the intent of building trust. In realising the paradox, Adam was able to own his part in the situation and reconnect with his desire to change and take action.

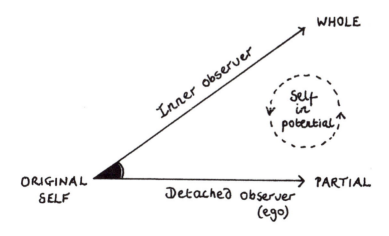

Figure 15

Paradox is a circuit maker. It is a reflection of our deeper nature and is a gateway to original self. In meeting with original self we make our acquaintance with the secret identity of the masterful coach. The interrelationship of these three different identities and aspects of self, and the capacity to coach, is illustrated in Figure 15, p.141.

Chapter Seven

THE ROLES OF THE COACH

...

In extending one's vision, the role of the coach evolves. This chapter examines a spectrum of the contrasting roles we adopt when we coach in moving from the analytical to the appreciative and creative eyes, including clarifier, conductor and co-creator. The evolution of this role is limited only by the imagination of the masterful coach.

...

The role of the coach is not fixed, but changes quite dramatically, depending on the viewpoint we take.

As the coach learns how to expand their vision, their role evolves

If we confine our vision or believe our role is fixed, then we can devalue the scope and possibility of coaching. When we discover the masterful coach we also find the exceptional vision of the creative eye. Let's remind ourselves of the composite nature of this eye (see Figure 16, below) and how it informs the different roles that the masterful coach plays in practice.

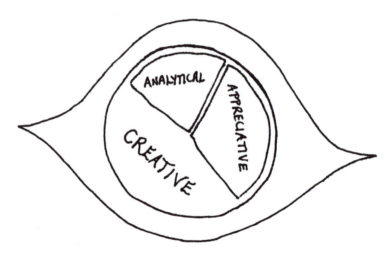

Figure 16

• THE ANALYTICAL ASPECT OF THE CREATIVE EYE •

I recently worked with a group of qualified counsellors and coaches who wished to explore and develop their coaching practice. I presented to the group concept of the three eyes of the coach and how these eyes combine to offer masterful practice. We discussed how they saw the role of the coach from the perspective of the analytical eye, and this was the list of possible roles that the group identified: *trainer, instructor, problem-solver, controller, fixer, differentiator* and *clarifier*.

PAUSE POINT

Which of these roles do you personally identify with and employ when you coach? How do they specifically serve your practice?

From the analytical perspective, the coach is seen to be a rational expert who imparts knowledge and information through instruction. We have already discussed how the analytical eye, when employed alone, can limit our potential to coach. This is because of the tendency of the instructor, for example, to want to fix rather than allowing the client the vital opportunity to find their own answers.

When the analytical aspect is combined and employed within the creative eye, it is much less reactive and more responsive. Here it provides a vital role to the work of the coach. Having helped the client to expand their awareness, the role of the clarifier is essential to the work of the coach. In every case study I have shared, you will note how, having employed the mirror to expand awareness, the lens of the creative eye is then vital to bring clarity and focus. Let me give you an example of the importance of the role of clarifier from a recent coaching conversation.

Philip is a senior physician within a major organisation. As he is being challenged by the complex matrix nature of his international role and the apparent lack of clarity around accountability, he sought help from a coach.

Philip: In the matrix I'm not clear about who is accountable for what.

Coach: What is the result?

I am using the mirror to expand awareness.

Philip:	Confusion (*pause*). Things don't get done.
Coach:	Anything more?
Philip:	Fear, there's a lot of fear.
Coach:	Anything more?
Philip:	Mmm (*pause*). A lot of protecting your own back, rather than getting the work done.
Coach:	How does this affect you personally?
Philip:	I'm frustrated and sometimes disappointed in myself.
Coach:	How come?
Philip:	I've begun to the play the game – to protect my back and not take accountability.
Coach:	How does that affect you?
Philip:	My motivation is dwindling.
Coach:	You seem a little down.
Philip:	I've taken the easy way out at times and it's crossing me – my true values.
Coach:	What values are being crossed?
Philip:	My integrity, fairness and the importance of taking personal accountability for things.

Having expanded awareness using the mirror, I now employ the analytical aspect of my vision – the lens – to help to clarify and determine the next steps.

Coach:	What are you learning from today?
Philip:	I think it's important to have heard myself say what I have said.
Coach:	Yes, you've been very honest with yourself and courageous to speak so openly.
Philip:	Something has to change.
Coach:	Ideally, what might that be?

Philip:	I'm going to discuss the real issue – accountability and fear – with some of my colleagues to see if we can put on the table how we might move this forward together.
Coach:	How and when might you do this?
Philip:	I'm meeting some of my key colleagues this week. I think I'll do it after the conference at the bar maybe. I need a comfortable, relaxed setting. I'll speak to two or three people and get a measure of whether they are struggling with the same issues as I am. I think they must be.
Coach:	What do you need to help you to make this happen?
Philip:	(*Pause*) Nothing. I've realised today that I need to do something for myself. I'm ready to move this forward. I have to for myself.
Coach:	What would your ultimate outcome be?
Philip:	Erm (*pause*). A meeting where we put all our issues on the table, name our fears and put things in place that free us to do our jobs much better.
Coach:	Are you committed to do this?
Philip:	Yes – I've got my motivation back.

In this example you can see the importance of the role of the clarifier. The key aspects having been brought into awareness are then refined and distilled. The outcomes and next steps are brought into clearer focus, grounded and crystallised. Note how, alone, the analytical eye can profoundly limit the work of the coach, whereas in combination it provides an essential aspect of all coaching practice. In my own experience the role of clarifier is essential to ground the new awareness of the client and determine the next key steps.

• THE APPRECIATIVE ASPECT OF THE CREATIVE EYE •

Recall the nature of the appreciative eye, the work of the inner observer and the value of the mirror. Let me share with you how, having discussed the nature of the appreciative eye, the same group described the roles of the coach from this perspective as: *enabler, awakener, wayfarer, catalyst, conductor, facilitator, integrator, harmoniser, energiser, carer* and *supporter*.

PAUSE POINT

Which role or roles do you personally employ when you coach and how do these serve you?

From the list there are three roles that are prominent in my own mind when I coach with the perspective of the appreciative eye. These are the wayfarer, conductor and carer. Let me illustrate their particular value to my own practice.

THE WAYFARER

The wayfarer is an important aspect of my conscience, helping me to remember why I coach. The wayfarer in me is willing to enter into the journey and adventure of coaching. One of my favourite wayfarers is Jason, of *Jason and the Argonauts* fame. Like Jason, when I coach I employ an enterprising eye and a willingness to enter courageously into the unknown as an adventure. Coaching takes courage and resilience.

TO BOLDLY GO

I often view the beginning of a new coaching relationship as an adventure. I remember the journey of the starship *Enterprise*. Its mission, you are likely to remember, is 'to boldly go where no man has gone before'. This starship ventures into the undiscovered expanse of outer space. The coach faces a similar adventure and challenge – not into outer space but more into inner space. When I think of the wayfarer, I am reminded that an important part of the journey of the coach is to be willing to explore the interior world of subjective experience, a world that the rational and concrete mind labels and fears as 'the unknown'.

THE ADVENTURE OF NOT KNOWING

The coach as a wayfarer is willing to enter into the unknown to help to guide their own and their client's learning and growth. Commonly when I coach I find myself in a place of not knowing: not knowing what's happening in the coaching relationship, not knowing what my client is truly wanting or needing, not knowing where to go next. It is important that we realise that the experience of not knowing is a vital aspect of the coaching process and does not reflect ineptitude in any way, quite the opposite.

It is in these moments I remember the coach is indeed a wayfarer.

> I can choose not to know as a means of fostering the growth of my clients

When I do this, I am able to give my full attention to the needs of the client rather than become anxious or fear that I am lost. The coach needs to be willing and able to stand beside the clients at their most challenging times – at the crossroads – and to enter willingly into uncertainty with endless curiosity.

When I coach, I coach myself to remember the value of not knowing the answer, for here is the chance to relate more deeply with my clients and to help them to discover their own answers.

If, when we coach, we can step into the place of not knowing then, in that moment, we create the possibility for our clients to remember their deeper desire, and motivation, to change. Maybe this is one of the most important gifts we can offer – to be willing to stay and walk beside our clients, not knowing the answer, but caring enough to stay present and attentive to their needs rather than our own. This capacity and quality of relationship is an essential part of the process of how we learn and develop. Once more, I am reminded of this when I think of the role of the wayfarer and my work as a coach.

MEETING THE MONSTERS

Might a key part of the coaching journey be a willingness to face and meet with our fears? We may often make monsters of ourselves. Let me explain.

We often judge and reject parts of ourselves when trying to meet other people's expectations. Some parts are labelled as bad and are banished to the edge of our awareness and beyond. In fearing these aspects of ourselves we make monsters of them. As we disown them, they appear alien and larger than life. The only option we seem to have is to fight them. I often recall how Jason always seemed to be fighting some larger-than-life monster on his journey.

But rather than fight, the coach is willing to meet with such monsters, to see them as rejected, lost and unwanted aspects of ourselves. If you are able to do this, then experiences find their true proportion. If allowed their rightful place, and we can meet with and accept them, then our apparent monsters no longer distort our self-perception or skew reality. This determination to face our fears and own our monsters is central to the work of the coach: in this way, we permit our clients the same prospect and possibility.

THE CONDUCTOR

When I coach it is valuable to remember the role of the conductor. The eye of the conductor tries to see and know all the parts of the orchestra. Although there can be solo instruments in an orchestra, the goal of the conductor is to harmonise. Generally, under the watchful eye of the conductor, there are no dominating divas. Through the work of the conductor the coach can begin to conceive of the orchestrated whole of which we are a part.

When I coach from the role of conductor, I remember my ability to stand apart and orchestrate. I have a clearer view of the different characters and instruments that comprise the orchestra (myself and my clients) and I can help to harmonise. The eye of the conductor is an integrative eye; it recognises and acknowledges the valuable contribution of each part and its relationship within the whole. Let me share an example of how the conductor can play a key role in coaching practice.

While I was demonstrating the possibilities of coaching to a group of new coaches, a client, David, presented a dilemma. David had checked into the group that morning having said that something quite wonderful had happened. He had returned from holiday where he had met some old friends. He had found himself working as a coach with two of these friends on separate occasions. Individually both had acknowledged how important and valuable conversations with David had been. Here is an excerpt from our coaching conversation:

David: There are two parts to me.
Coach: Tell me more.

David:	One is a part that really needs to work hard. The other is a part that just wants to step back and take time out.
Coach:	How does that make you feel?
David:	Caught, stuck. I have to work hard because that is what one has to do for a living. If I step back I feel guilty.
Coach:	Recall what you checked in with this morning.
David:	Mm (*pause*). Yes.
Coach:	What I took from that, was that it seems that your real work is happening when you are on vacation, when you are relaxed and stepping back.
David:	(*Laughs*) That's true, I suppose. But that's not hard work. I need to work hard.

My conductor steps in to orchestrate the proceedings from here. David's eyes see a further possibility other than the 'either, or' that is being played out.

Coach:	Maybe you can have it all?
David:	How?
Coach:	How can you meet the needs of both, rather than thinking you need to go 'either, or'?
David:	Mmm (*pause*).
Coach:	Can you allow your good work to continue when you step back and also find a way of satisfying that part of you that needs to work hard?
David:	Maybe (*pause*). Maybe I can – strange, I'd never thought of that possibility
Coach:	Maybe you can have it all?

When the conductor steps into the frame, I realise the value in orchestration. In this case there is a duet, rather than the dilemma of choosing between two soloists.

THE CARER

When I take the role of carer as a coach, I adopt a more relational and empathic position. This often makes me wonder if the appreciative eye is common to the caring professions. Is the role of carer employed in the professions of counselling, mentoring, psychotherapy and nursing practice, to mention but a few?

I have often heard it said that the higher one climbs the ladder of business success, the lonelier the experience. The capacity to care forms an essential part of coaching; it is fashioned through self-acceptance and demonstrated in how we encourage, support and guide others.

The carer reminds me of the importance of remembering 'how we are' in 'what we do'

Caring and the capacity to empathise bring a vital quality to the coaching relationship. Such qualities often need no words to be deeply felt and can profoundly influence how we coach.

I feel privileged when a client is able to share and include their emotions in the coaching relationship. From my own experience, and from speaking with other coaches, the fear of feelings is often a fear of being overwhelmed by them and being unable to contain them. Remember, if we deny our emotions they can easily take super-human dimensions. We can unwittingly make monsters of what has normal human proportion.

We have explored how, with the opening of the creative eye, the coach can learn how to simply witness, meet with and experience emotions. A strong, stable inner reference and guide fosters self-acceptance and deepens our awareness of our own psychology.

The following excerpt demonstrates the role of the coach as carer – accepting, managing and containing the emotions of the client.

Mandy is a manager and leader. In our first session, having set the coaching frame, Mandy checks in:

Client: I'm Mandy and I'm a manager and I have a number of staff and I find it challenging work as there is always something going on that I seem to miss and it's important for me to have coaching right now and I want to explore quite a few things but I'm not sure where to begin and I've got some things going on in the group and . . .

There were no full stops, no breathing spaces and I was feeling as though I couldn't breathe. I checked in with myself and decided to playfully intervene and mirror my experience.

Coach: Mandy, dear Mandy, I am feeling exhausted and I've only been with you a few minutes. Are you allowed to take a breath or use a full stop (*smile*)? Phew! (*Mandy looks at me and smiles shyly.*) When did you last take a break (*smile*)?

Mandy: Is it that bad?

Coach: It's not bad at all. I just can't keep up when you speak fast and without punctuation. I feel lost and a little exhausted (*pause*). Is this a good place for us to work?

Mandy: Yes, I think so.

I still can't get my breath back and so decide the following step.

Coach: Mandy, would you be willing to stop with me
            for a moment, so that we can just breathe
            together? Is that OK?

Mandy: Yes.

*Mandy stops and we just take a few deep breaths together. As
Mandy takes several deep breaths in and out she bursts into
tears. My heart opens as I see what may be sitting beneath her
activity.*

Coach: It's OK Mandy, I am with you.

*We continue just to breathe together – while smiling and reassuring
her that it's fine just to be here.*

Coach: So, Mandy, share a little more if you're willing
            about what's going on for you. Help me to
            understand.

Mandy: I'm not sure. When I get here I feel so lost. I'm
            tired and exhausted.

Note how this mirrors my own experience.

Coach: I'm not surprised. I wonder when the last time
            was that you truly stopped and breathed. You
            may not have been here for a while, so it's not
            surprising that you may at first feel lost.

Mandy: Mmm. It's true (*pause*).

Coach: Just take what time you might need.

Mandy: Yes.

Coach: Are you OK to work here? Is this the right
            place for you?

Reminding Mandy about her choice is important – it places the power to decide back in her hands.

Mandy: Yes, I know this is important. But I don't
              understand what's going on when I get here
              and whenever I stop talking I become emotional
              and often cry.

Coach: Is that so?

Mandy's feelings are overwhelming her. It may have been a while since she was last in touch.

Mandy: Yes.

Coach: Might there be something important here for
              you?

Mandy: Yes. I might remember something I've for-
              gotten.

Coach: Maybe.

Mandy: I know this is important for me to work here –
              this does affect me so much in my work and
              home. Is there another way I can work with
              this to understand what's happening a little
              more?

I hear the request for help. I return to my inner compass and guide and reflect and realise that I am very much still aware of the lack of breath. I decide that this may be useful and a positive context to work with Mandy. I don't want to take Mandy away from her feelings and emotions, but I also don't want her to feel so overwhelmed at being here. Is there a way she may make more sense of this experience? So I decide to plant a seed.

Coach: Maybe. Let me plant a seed and see what you
              think. I experience you as talking super fast

(*we smile*). There are no pauses and no full
stops when you talk. I'm curious if your life
and work has any grammar or punctuation,
even a comma now and then (*we both laugh*).
Have you ever thought what your breathing
represents?

Mandy: No.

Coach: Well, to breathe in is to do what?

Mandy: I'm not sure (*pause*). Tell me.

Coach: It's to inspire. The in-breath is the inspiration
and the out-breath is to expire. In moving so
fast, I wonder if you may be missing your inspiration.

Mandy: Wow, how interesting!

Coach: To get to what inspires, you may be able to get
to know your feelings a little more?

Mandy: Mmm. That's so interesting. I am always
looking to other people for direction and the
answer. I never do look to myself for that.

Mandy seems to have forgotten her own inner compass and looks to others for direction.

Coach: That's an interesting realisation, isn't it
Mandy? If you're forgetting to breathe, try to
remember what inspires you. Be curious,
explore and consider what you desire to do.
Begin to set your own direction. Will you try
this and practise?

Mandy: Yes I will. I think this is spot on.

Coach: This is our first session but might this be an
interesting theme for our work, I wonder?

Mandy:	Yes, definitely.
Coach:	Are you OK if I remind you of your speed and breathing when we work together so that we can pace things?
Mandy:	Yes, that would be helpful.

This turned out to be a very interesting theme to our work. This context provided a meaningful way in which Mandy could be in what seemed like a difficult place. Even after one session Mandy began more consciously to manage the pace of how she was speaking and her breathing. She explored what it was like to add pauses and punctuation to her working life and began to remember and realise what inspires. Gradually she moved from running away from her subjective experience – her feelings and inspiration – to being able to trust and rely on these for guidance and direction. This personal change impacted both her work and her personal life.

> If, when we coach, we are unable to meet with our own feelings, then we do not permit our clients the chance to explore this possibility for themselves

Note the importance of being able to provide a context, when working with emotions, that gives the clients' emotions value and place – particularly with difficult emotions. When I coach I like to remind myself of the importance of the role of the carer and the associated integrative and appreciative eye that is willing to include and accept all feelings – my own and those of my clients.

• THE ROLE OF THE COACH AS SEEN FROM THE CREATIVE EYE •

The group collectively identified the following descriptions of the role of the coach as seen from this viewpoint of the creative eye: *guide, gardener, reframer, transformer, resolver, a mix of artist and scientist, negotiator, mediator, synthesiser* and *co-creator.*

PAUSE POINT

Which role or roles do you personally employ when you coach and how does this serve you?

Let me share with you how I mindfully employ the work of the roles of the gardener, co-creator and resolver when I coach.

THE GARDENER

I am a keen gardener and love to plant seeds. Before I do, I carefully prepare the ground and ask the questions: 'Is it the right time to plant?' and 'Are the conditions ideal for growth?' As a gardener I have to consider what is likely to nourish and encourage the growth of the seed. Is the soil fertile, are the weather and seasonal conditions good, and is the aspect right? The very best I can do is seek to lovingly nurture the growth of the seed. I cannot make the seed grow, as its actual growth is out of my hands and beyond my responsibility. No matter how much I might care and long for the seed to grow, which is my clear intention, the actual growth of the seed depends on its own resilience and inner resourcefulness and the impact and influence of wider nature.

This is an important lesson for the coach and something we need always to remember. The actual growth of your client is not your direct responsibility and is out of your hands. We can guide and help to facilitate growth but we are not responsible for our client's actual growth.

The more we take responsibility, the less impact we can potentially make

This marks the true domain of influence of the coach.

When I coach, I do plant seeds and will openly say in my coaching conversations, 'Might I plant a seed for you to consider?' as you have seen in the case studies. The seeds I plant when coaching set the prospect and potential for the client to develop. Planting a seed often highlights a new way of looking at something, from which the client can learn and develop. If the client understands and learns from the value of this reframe, then the seed begins to grow.

Let me give you an example from a previous case study in Chapter 3. Susan, as you may recall, is an experienced coach who is struggling with an issue around the concepts of 'doing' and 'being'. She loves the activity of doing. It is an integral part of her life. She has never felt able to work with the concept of being because she believes that to do so she would have to slow down and stop doing – which is something she feels she couldn't do. I realise how doing and being have been split, and so I plant a seed.

Coach:	Susan, let me plant a seed. When you talk about being and doing you separate the two. Doing is moving, being is still. How would it be to consider a third way? What if your being was in your doing? What if you could find perfect stillness and being within every busy moment?
Susan:	Mmm. So that I'm present to the moment in all that I do?
Coach:	Yes. It may not be 'either, or' but allowing yourself to experience 'both'.
Susan:	Yes. Mmm (*laughing*).
Coach:	Might it not be as black and white as you think?
Susan:	I'm always trying to separate things. So the seed that you plant for me to consider is that

	being and doing can be one and the same – the being in the doing? Mmm (*pause*).
Coach:	Yes. Maybe the more we make the being a destiny, the more it becomes out of our reach. What do you think?
Susan:	Maybe (*long pause.*) Yes.

I am not giving Susan the answer here, I am providing a reframe in which she can potentially learn and grow. The reframe gives her an opportunity to extend her awareness and understand beyond her current belief system. When planted, this seed continued to grow over the following month. Susan returned to the next coaching session having acknowledged her being in her doing and was applying this learning to her coaching practice. The seed was planted and, in this case, it grew quickly.

The seed does not always grow so quickly. If the seed does not grow it is not for you to worry – all we can do when we coach is decide the right time and conditions to plant the seed and nourish it to the best of our ability. It is important the coach does not feel responsible for the client's growth. All we can do is plant seeds. Some may fall on stony ground. Let me share a short story that I read in a newspaper some years ago that I hope you will carry with you when you coach.

A team of gardeners from Kew, one of the main horticultural centres in the UK, were researching rare seeds. They had, according to the report, found such a seed within a burial ground and cave. They collected this seed and began to explore if they could nurture its germination and growth. With care and patience they did just that, and the seed began to germinate and grow. The seed that germinated was in fact 1,500 years old!

I find this a remarkable story and valuable to the coach. The seeds we plant may not germinate and grow immediately. They may remain latent until the conditions for growth are more ideal. The best you can do as a coach and gardener is to plant your seed well, with care, thought and intentionality: the rest is truly out of our hands. Conscious growth is a desire that the client chooses to fulfil. It cannot be forced; if it is, the potential for growth is immediately lost.

THE CO-CREATOR

The work of the gardener and the co-creator are quite closely related. Both offer valuable insights to the role of the coach. The gardener does not garden alone – growth involves the seed, the gardener and wider nature. Growth is quite an intimate and relational affair.

In Spain, my farmhouse is surrounded by cork oak forest. These trees are ancient, and some are many hundreds of years old. Every year they drop their acorns. Often I will pick up an acorn and wonder, how in heaven's name does the acorn become an oak tree? How are our journeys encoded in something so small, and can yet create the beauty of something so large? Such questions mark the curiosity of the coach interested in the process of creativity and creation.

Are we like the acorn and dream of becoming an oak? Maybe we all long to be, and to become, something more. The self, as we have explored, is not fixed but an emerging concept. It is the work of the coach to create chances for the clients to move closer towards becoming the individuals they were born to be. Through the coaching relationship a client can discover, and in fact create, this person. The coach, culture and wider nature are all potential architects who can potentially help to affirm, define, discover and create identity, so we are co-creators.

> ## Through the work of the coach we evoke and give form and expression to our deepest humanity – the universal and original being

Might this be the seed of our longing and the fruition of our journey, and indeed the masterful coach? When I coach I often remember the importance of co-creation and the chance this offers my clients for self-discovery.

THE RESOLVER

When I coach I also often remember the importance of my role as a resolver. Let's explore how and why this role is particularly important to the coach and how this capacity develops together with the opening of the creative eye.

The analytical eye is keen to answer, the appreciative eye is curious to question, and the creative eye is simply free to respond. The creative eye can expand and question, contract and answer, and also simply contemplate the unanswered question. Let me explain and illustrate the importance of this a little more fully, for this enables the coach to truly resolve.

The vision of the creative eye is able to see and witness conflict – essentially how the analytical eye makes judgements and divides and splits. Rather than being drawn into the conflict of choosing one side or the other, the creative eye is able to consider both sides equally. This is the unconditional eye of the negotiator, it can see and accept both sides without being drawn into either. Rather than seeking to immediately solve, it looks beneath to discover the unanswered question. This unanswered question is to be found at the heart of conflict and division and has the potential to offer new insight and growth and a deeper, more creative resolution.

Another way of seeing this is that the creative eye is comfortable with paradox and dilemma. It is comfortable with its own paradoxical nature and can acknowledge the paradox of things. It is not tempted to reductively simplify or solve; it is able simply to observe, contemplate and reflect.

The example I gave earlier in the role of the gardener with Susan also offers insight into the role of the coach as a resolver. Susan was caught into believing that she had to choose either this or that. In essence, I am good at doing but can't do being, because I love activity. The creative eye can weigh the value of both equally and provide the reframe. Rather than either being or doing, I explored whether Susan could discover her being in every moment of her activity – that is, in her doing. In this way the creative eye and its instrumentation provide the coach with the balance, patience and unconditional care to discover the unanswered question that sits beneath the conflict.

In discovering the masterful coach rather than seeking to reductively solve and simplify, we can sensitively explore a deeper and potentially more creative resolution.

Rather than seek an answer, the masterful coach seeks the unanswered question

Einstein once stated in essence that you can't solve the problem by the same logic that created it. The coach as a resolver knows this to be true and is able to guide the client to look beyond the immediacy of the presented conflict to explore if there is a deeper resolution. When I coach and find myself facing conflict,

I remember the role of the resolver and begin to weigh both sides, patiently looking deeper for the yet unanswered question and the chance of a more creative and peaceful resolution.

• THE MANY ROLES OF THE COACH •

Though we often speak of the role of the coach as if it were singular, we have explored how it has an innate plurality, as illustrated in Figure 17, below.

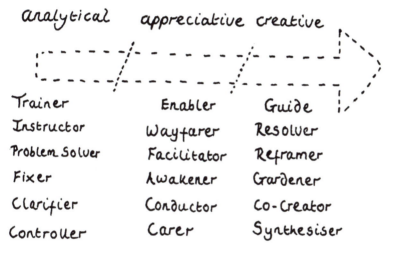

analytical	appreciative	creative
Trainer	Enabler	Guide
Instructor	Wayfarer	Resolver
Problem Solver	Facilitator	Reframer
Fixer	Awakener	Gardener
Clarifier	Conductor	Co-Creator
Controller	Carer	Synthesiser

The Emerging Role of the Coach.

Figure 17

As we open different eyes, discover our inner instrumentation and adopt different identities – ultimately discovering the masterful coach – the roles of the coach evolve and emerge, giving us an insight into the true scope of our occupation. The next time you coach, keep a watchful eye on how many different roles you take on in each coaching session and those that pre-dominate in your own practice. As we discover the imagination of the masterful coach, we continue to shape and evolve the role of the coach and the scope and field of coaching.

Chapter Eight

BEING AND BECOMING MASTERFUL

• • •

Now we will explore the nature of masterful coaching practice and the experience of being, play, not knowing, impartiality, holding and flow. Also, how the faculties of intention, intuition, imagination and integrity emerge together with qualities such as compassion to inform the presence of the masterful coach.

• • •

We seem to look everywhere else for the key to mastery except in our own hands.

You and no one else hold the key to your masterful practice right here, right now; the master key is already in your hands

• ENDING THE SEARCH •

The more we *try* to coach, the less our success. Mastery is found when you realise that there is nothing more you need to find. Mastery is the confidence and self-reliance that you discover when you place your trust in your own natural and innate ability to coach. When you permit yourself the freedom of not striving, you can begin to experience and enjoy these talents and discover and employ the essential inner toolkit of the masterful coach.

It is a fascinating revelation to the coach that we can spend our whole lives searching for mastery, only to realise that being masterful is the natural consequence of ending our need to search.

• ACCEPTING FALLIBILITY •

To end your need to search and start your progress to mastery, there are certain things you must allow yourself to be, or allow into your life, and being fallible is one of them.

While writing this book I accepted an opportunity to teach a group of counsellors and psychotherapists who wished to explore coaching practice. The details of this workshop, which was to run over three months, were set and advertised.

One morning, out of the blue (or so I thought), the course director called. He asked very anxiously, 'Where are you?' 'At home', I replied. A part of me froze with his next comment: 'Andrew, your students are waiting for you!'

To my horror I had by mistake put the wrong date in my diary and the course had started without me! My students were waiting and some had travelled long distances to attend. On a scale of 1 to 10 of nightmare situations, I experienced this to be about an 8.

We worked out a strategy where the director would ask the students whether they were willing to start the course the following day. If so, I would drive to London immediately. As I put the phone down, I started a process of self-reproach and felt simply mortified by my error. I couldn't quite believe how I had got this so wrong.

The director returned thirty minutes later to say that all the students were willing to begin the course the next day. So my journey down to London began. Only when I was in my car and breathing more deeply did I begin to reflect and consider what might be happening.

Over twenty years of coaching, I could not recall missing an appointment and yet I had got this date completely wrong. Might this error in some way be important and could it inform my teaching of the course?

The next morning I woke very early, to be absolutely sure that I would be there on time. The moment arrived when my participants entered the room. I started:

> Let me begin by saying how truly, truly sorry I am about yesterday. It was entirely my error and I realise that I left you stranded here as a result. I am truly sorry about that and I am grateful for your willingness and flexibility to work today and tomorrow. When I realised my mistake, I was over four hours' drive away. Once more, please accept my sincere apology.

I took time to explore how my absence had impacted each person and then turned to the group and expressed clearly:

> This experience has brought me in close touch with my own fallibility. I wonder how important fallibility is to the

work of the coach? Might we consider this as an important context to the course over the next three months, since its presence is so visible as we begin?

And so we did, and what an insightful context it turned out to be.

We drew the illuminating conclusion together:

When we accept our fallibility, our limitation, our imperfection, we no longer strive to become someone other than our most natural self. We are free and can relax into the discovery of a deeper centre of identity – the original self – and it is there that we can meet with the masterful coach.

Fallibility takes comfort in imperfection and finds joy and wonder in the ordinary. Acceptance is the key that can unlock and free your mastery.

Maybe the masterful coach is your most authentic identity as a human being

FALLIBILITY AND THE ORGANISATIONAL COACH

The permission to be fallible may at first seem at odds with the demands of high-level business. The need of organisations is for employees to access more of their hidden potential and resourcefulness to become increasingly productive – often I will hear the leadership message, 'We need to do more with the same or less'. Underlying this message is a fear of making mistakes. Mistakes are no longer permitted. But being infallible and not being permitted mistakes are inconceivable. Only when we accept our fallibility does striving end and a door inwardly open, through which we can explore and access our inner resourcefulness and so help others to do the same.

We can now see how the invincible and infallible analytical eye imprisons its own potential and creative possibility. Only when the analytical aspect is combined with the appreciative to form the creative eye can it see beyond its own blindness. This is the way we can unlock the unlimited potential of the masterful coach.

PAUSE POINT

Consider the consequences of accepting your fallibility as a coach. How does your fallibility actually inform your practice?

• EXPERIENCE OF MASTERY •

How can we describe and discern mastery? I think of mastery as something similar to discovering a secret recipe. We suddenly realise the vital ingredients that combine together to offer masterful practice.

BEING

We have already considered how, in striving continually to get somewhere else or to be someone else, we create the experience of an isolated, partial and incomplete self. The masterful coach realises that, in searching for something more outside ourselves, we lose sight of something vital within – the source from which our power to change originates. When we can end our need to search, we realise the full possibility and prospect of the present moment.

In striving to remember the past or visioning the possibility of the future, we actually lose our concentration and attentiveness, and the present moment can pass us by. The present moment is the only place we can change; past and future are virtual realities. We cannot choose from any other place but the present moment. In fact, this is all we ever have – I think of it sometimes as my ever-present now.

For the masterful coach, every moment is fulfilling and a destiny in itself. Making each moment a destiny in itself, we focus our vision on the here and now. What we learn is how to savour and notice things that previously we would have missed. We become the most attentive, playful and deeply caring observer, a lover of watching and listening. When we surrender our need to be someone else or somewhere else, we begin to remember the original self and recognise the true identity of the masterful coach.

PLAY

Have you noticed how the best questions seem to be asked by children, with their endless curiosity about themselves and the world around? A child is spontaneous and has no uneasy hesitation; questions are asked openly and honestly. Children have a freedom that is commonly lost to the adult. Their creativity is unbounded and a joy to observe.

My great niece Millie came to my house to play. Millie is six years old. While we were in the garden, Millie decided to dance and sing me a song. She took hold of the sweeping brush as a microphone and proceeded to dance and sing (her own composition) on the theme of tulips.

I was astonished and marvelled at her creativity, sense of freedom and enjoyment. There was no hesitation with words or rhymes, everything just flowed. She danced freely as she sang, loving the whole experience. I noted how endearing she was in her sense of freedom and play. Through her rendition I reconnected with the importance of the child to the work of the masterful coach. The coach can learn a great deal from children and, in the course of the coaching journey, I believe we often do.

When I coach I am often reminded of the child within me, who is keen to play and be free, inviting me to share in this experience. This is not a childish presence. Through the innocent eyes of my child I seem to see the world afresh. My sense of humour and fun are awakened, and there is endless curiosity and questioning. No question in fact seems out of bounds, and I feel a sense of wonder. I can more deeply appreciate the beauty of ordinary things. I am often spontaneous and highly intuitive.

PAUSE POINT

Imagine the value of the child to your work as a coach. Do you ever free the child when you practise?

The freedom, curiosity and playfulness of the child are important traits associated with the discovery of the masterful coach

My playful child and compassionate adult can be a very powerful and insightful partnership. When I coach I can give challenging feedback with humour, honesty, care and a lightness of touch. Let me share a few recent examples from my own coaching practice.

The adult can often have a great hesitancy around what one should do, or must do, that is absent from the child. When I coach, mindful of the child and the importance of play, I seize that endearing honesty and playfulness and often feel inspired to act in the moment.

I was working recently in a group supervision setting with a number of coaches. I realised that one member of the group, Paul, was dominant and a little intimidating. I wondered how this aspect of Paul's persona might influence his coaching relationships. While working with the group, I suddenly turned to Paul.

Coach: Paul, do you know you are a bit scary (*laughing*)? Has anyone ever told you that before (*laughing*)?

Paul: (*Laughing also*) No, am I really?

Coach: Yes, just a touch, just a smidgen.

I feel playful and quite spontaneous in giving this important feedback. John, another member of the group, intervenes.

John: You are a bit (*smiling*).

Paul: I didn't realise. Might I scare my clients?

Coach: You might, I don't know (*smiling*). What do you think?

Paul: I need to explore this, I think.

Coach: Good. We can let you know if we experience you as scary, if that would help, can't we folks? This may help you to get to know that part of yourself a little better – more consciously maybe. Does that work for you?

Paul: Yes that would be helpful.

Paul did some good work getting to know this dominant characteristic of his persona. As he recognised this aspect, the group observed and mirrored how Paul's persona softened.

NOT KNOWING

We seem to believe that life is a search for the answer and yet the single most important revelation leading to the discovery of the masterful coach is how, in cultivating the capacity to not know, we can remember our motivation to change and realise our creative potential and possibility.

The masterful coach is quite comfortable in not having to know the answer. Normally this experience of not knowing causes anxiety, fear and sometimes panic. From my experience, our capacity for not knowing is key to development and growth. Paradoxically, not knowing provides the client with the chance to expand awareness, discover new choices and accept creative insights. In the coaching relationship, the client can practise not knowing with someone trustworthy. This is a vital opportunity for learning and growth.

By being present to another, to walk beside or guide someone else, to truly help another to develop and grow, we are invited to let go of knowing and having the answer.

> It is a courageous act to share not knowing with someone else to help them to rediscover their desire to change and grow

It is an act of faith where we decide to get lost together, trusting that the answer will emerge from within through the courage and freedom of not having to know.

In Chapter 7 we explored the different roles of the coach, and one in particular again comes to mind – the wayfarer. When you coach you take an adventure with someone else – you decide to enter into the unknown in order to potentially help another to grow. The masterful coach is certainly a wayfarer: someone who is willing to enter wholeheartedly into the adventure of not knowing, paradoxically in order to know something more about the generative nature of self and the coaching relationship. In our willingness to explore, we help our clients to forget who they think they are and instead discover who they might truly be.

• IMPARTIALITY •

Most of the case studies I have included show how we and our clients commonly get stuck and are unable to choose a way forward. We somehow get caught in the duality we create. The masterful coach can clearly see and yet not react to division, duality and difference. This parallels the ability of the coach to accommodate the paradoxical nature of reality. Let us explore in more detail what I mean by this.

The masterful eye is an impartial eye. It can look at either this or that and consider the pros and cons. It can also see, sense and articulate a deeper, often hidden, relationship between apparently contradictory elements. This offers the masterful coach the rare ability to contextualise. The vision of the masterful coach can sometimes see and conceive of the larger whole in which the client's experience is a part. It is the work of the masterful coach to conceive and discover these larger contexts to offer the clients the chance to understand more deeply their apparent dilemma, to make meaning of their journey, and to grow.

When I coach, I gradually see how a client may be limiting their vision and potential by judging and dividing – wanting either this or that. I will often smile and plant the seed: 'Have you considered if you might be able to have it all?' Providing the larger context – naming the paradox and reframing the current situation and scenario – is once more not about giving the client the answer. Instead, it helps the client to see the potential and possibility within the present moment. In realising our potentiality we remember our innate mobility and desire to change.

When I plant seeds it is an invitation to the client to discover, through the shared eyes of the coaching relationship, a larger context that may bring learning, development and meaning to their journey. This essentially provides an opportunity for the client to step beyond division and conflict to consider if there is a deeper, more creative and meaningful resolution. In discovering the masterful coach we can help the client to step out of conflict and reconnect with their innate desire to change and grow.

> The coach reminds the client of their potentiality and can transform a sense of 'feeling stuck' into the prospect of mobility and desired change

Let me demonstrate what I mean by recalling an earlier case study.

Susan, you may remember, has a dilemma of 'being' and 'doing'. Susan's temptation was to split these twins and to focus on either being or doing. Having weighed up both, her favoured choice was doing, because this allowed her the joy of activity. Her moment of realisation happened when the seed was planted that she might be able to 'have it all' – was there value and meaning in considering how her *being* may exist at all times within her *doing*?

Like the eye of a storm, do we find stillness within each busy moment? Rather than split, Susan was able to embrace her paradoxical nature – the being in her doing – and see the value and learning opportunity presented by this larger context. Her learning strongly influenced and informed her coaching practice as well as her personal development.

When we discover the masterful coach we can operate from a place within that is beyond duality and conflict. From this platform, rather than react to division and difference, the coach can offer the client impartiality – the unconditional opportunity to meet with and consider both sides equally. This allows the client to look beneath and beyond the immediate challenge to discover whether a deeper, more peaceful, resolution exists. It opens the possibility that if we can see past the temptation to judge and split, we can discover new potentiality and the prospect for growth. Through the shared eye of the masterful coach, apparent problems can transform into opportunities for development and growth, and provide the chance to discover a deeper and more meaningful context to our life and work.

The masterful coach reminds the client of the dynamic relationship and potentiality that can be realised by acknowledging our partial wholeness. We are singular in seeking to differentiate and see ourselves as distinct – apart from others. We are also plural in ever seeking to find our place and belonging – a part of something larger. This defines our innate and dynamic potentiality that motivates change (see Figure 18, opposite).

• HOLDING •

In moments of mastery we also discover a quality of holding. This is a capacity of the coach to recognise an aspect of which the client is unaware, and to purposefully hold this new awareness until the client is ready and able to accept it. The masterful coach knows the importance of timing and will consciously hold certain aspects of this potential gift until the time is right to share. Let me use a recent case study to illustrate this holding capacity.

Pat, a senior scientist and physician, was badly affected by profound organisational changes and a shifting role. Part of her behaviour showed a critical mistrust of authority. When

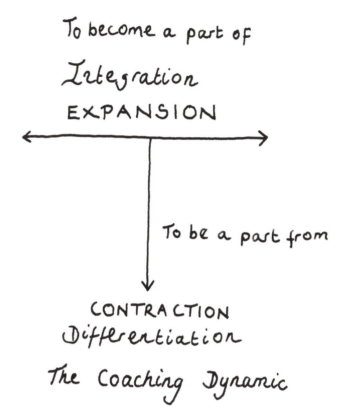

To become a part of

Integration

EXPANSION

To be a part from

CONTRACTION

Differentiation

The Coaching Dynamic

Figure 18

working with Pat, I chose to hold a particular piece of what I considered to be vital feedback for some months, until Pat was in a more generative and stable place, and was able to receive and work with this feedback. Consider the following extracts from my coaching conversation:

Coach: How are you now, Pat?
Pat: Better, more stable and engaging a little more.
Coach: On a scale of 1 to 10, where are you in your satisfaction with your current role?

Pat:	You asked me this last time and it was 2 or 3 – now it's 5 or 6.
Coach:	(*We smile*) What's changed?
Pat:	I have (*pause*). . . I feel with your help – I am more in control of my destiny.
Coach:	Are you in a good place to progress the coaching work?
Pat:	(*Laughs*) Yes.
Coach:	How do you feel about your boss or bosses now?
Pat:	I am beginning to engage more, but still keep on the edge.
Coach:	Is it safer there?
Pat:	Yes. I'm critical of strategy and don't fully buy in, so I don't fully engage.
Coach:	Good awareness. So you avoid fully engaging and step out of relationship?
Pat:	Yes.
Coach:	That keeps you safe?
Pat:	Yes.
Coach:	But you don't engage fully?
Pat:	No.
Coach:	Do you make a choice?
Pat:	No. I don't fully commit.
Coach:	How does this limit you, Pat?
Pat:	(*Pause*) I'm never fully committed (*pause*) or a part of anything really.
Coach:	There's something I want to bring to your attention.

I have checked in with myself and the time feels right to share back with Pat something that I have been holding for a while – the potential saboteur.

Pat:	Yes?
Coach:	Are you sabotaging something here? In keeping yourself safe, are you losing something quite precious?
Pat:	(*Long pause*) Mmm. I'm setting this up, aren't I?
Coach:	Say more.
Pat:	In not trusting, I think I do sabotage getting more involved and being a part of something – influencing things.
Pat:	Excellent Pat, your awareness is spot on. You appear to have a saboteur protector.

The saboteur is made conscious and given back into Pat's care. I am delighted to see how much Pat is gaining insight and awareness, and am keen to give her encouragement.

Pat:	That's useful. I am creating the same old sequence, aren't I, then blaming it on bad leadership?
Coach:	The leadership may play their part and, yes, you may be recreating something. What about the chance for you to shape your ideal job? Do you have a choice? If you're not engaged and willing to consider and value your own needs, how can you shape and potentially influence your future and your occupation?

This feels generative, so I explore how willing Pat may be to work with her choice and be able to shape her ideal role/occupation.

Pat:	(*Long pause*) I hadn't realised how much I have been limiting myself and that I have a choice to make it different.

| Coach: | You can change that now, if you desire? |
| Pat: | Yes (*pause*), I think it's the right time. |

The capacity to hold in this way is essential to the work of the coach. If we return to the coaching jigsaw analogy, we are making conscious and giving to the client what may be an important piece of the jigsaw that has been held in our care that may help to complete a section and resolve the puzzle – we are giving this back to the client as a gift.

The coach is effectively helping the client to come to know and accept different aspects of their personality. Authenticity can deepen as a result. After being quite traumatised by a sequence of events and dramatic change, Pat was now reflecting more deeply. She was expressing how her own psychological process was serving and limiting her work, becoming more honest with herself and realising her desire to change.

• FLOW •

When we discover the masterful coach we realise the paradox that mobility is the natural consequence of being and becoming still.

The activity of masterful coaching does not deplete energy but revitalises. When we discover the masterful coach and allow this presence to guide our coaching, we do not tire of practice and our energy levels remain topped up. Mastery happens when we realign with a centre and source of our potential for development and learning. We make the discovery of original self and recomplete a circuit whereby our hidden potential becomes available as power. This we experience as being in flow. As we return to our original nature we discover an innate energy – a will that literally moves us. We are inspired to respond spontaneously from the inside out.

The masterful coach can purely focus their attention on the activity of coaching. The activity is fulfilling in itself and serves no other purpose. The quality of relationship between coach and client naturally deepens. The prospect of flow becomes potentially available to the client, as both the client and the coach share the same energy field.

Two of my clients have described the experience of being in flow in coaching sessions. In order to ground learning and harness the potential value, I asked if they would describe this experience in words. Here are extracts taken from both transcripts that, I believe, help to illuminate the experience of being in flow and how this relates to mastery.

Ben is an experienced coach in supervision:

> My experience of being in flow is one where I feel I am being carried and inwardly directed. I respond without doubting or questioning. I act immediately in the moment. It's not difficult and does not involve rational thought or consideration. I don't weigh things up; the experience is spontaneous. There is some sort of inner knowing. It feels very easy, as if it were the easiest thing in the world really. I feel alive – an inner energy and force moves me.

Deborah is an experienced senior IT leader and manager in a multinational organisation:

> It's quite difficult to explain this experience of being in flow. It's a tangible feeling that things are happening in a positive way, with actions interlinking and events unfolding as time moves on. It doesn't feel like there is a predetermined pattern, but more like riding the crest of

> the wave and being simply able to take opportunities
> that come along as I am travelling forward. It feels like
> some sort of magical force is at play, which I have found
> a way to tap into, and it is giving me the ability to do
> more and see more than before.

Note how mastery involves little or no effort and it is an inspired activity. The masterful coach within is the source of our motivation to act and guide.

• THE EMERGING FACULTIES •

Discovering mastery seems to be characterised by the emergence of particular faculties – intention, intuition, imagination and integrity. These faculties begin to emerge into more conscious use with the opening of the creative eye and being at one with the inner compass. I often imagine each of these faculties aligning with the directions of the compass, as illustrated in Figure 19, opposite.

These faculties inform how we act and the direction we consciously take. They collectively combine to offer masterful practice and create a fifth faculty – *presence*.

INTENTION

The faculty of intention is a conscious setting of a clear direction in the mind of the coach. Setting intention provides the opportunity to plan our life and work in advance by consciously identifying, before we begin, what we would ideally like to happen.

Intention helps the coach to navigate and
to plot the way in advance

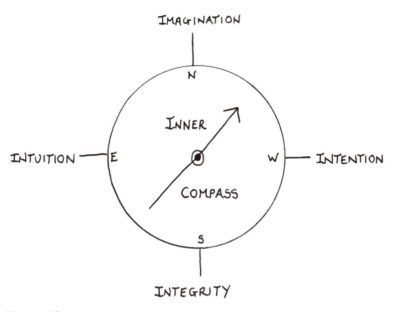

Figure 19

It provides the coach with clarity of purpose and direction. If intention is not consciously set, then we often fill the space with activity. We fire-fight and feel there is never enough time to complete our work. Intention is like a lamp we consciously light that can illuminate, remind and clarify each step of our journey.

When I begin to coach a client and set the coaching frame, I commonly make my intention clear to the client: 'I am committed to your development and helping you to fully realise your most desired change. You are my primary focus. You will have my full attention and support. I intend to get to know you well.' Being clear and stating my intention affirms not only my commitment and the intended direction of the work, but also what the client can expect of me.

An important part of the role of the coach is to help to clarify the intention of the client. This leads to questions such as: 'Remind me, where, ideally, would you like to get to with this?' 'If you could wave a magic wand, what would change for you?' 'What does realising your goal look and feel like?'

PAUSE POINT

How do you employ intention in your coaching practice? What is its specific value to your work?

In modelling the value of intention, the coach can help the client to realise its value. Let me share an example from a recent coaching session with Simon to illustrate this.

When we first met, Simon told me how he would often go into key business meetings quite unclear of what he needed or wanted. This created the sense of feeling lost and needing other people to set direction for him.

Simon: I think I'm quite needy, I need a lot of guidance.

I see how Simon turns to others for the answer and devalues his own ability to answer and set his own course.

Coach: Who do you trust to guide you?
Simon: (*Pause*) I always feel a little lost and need other people to give me direction.
Coach: There's probably only one person who knows what you truly want and where you would ideally like to get to, is that not true?
Simon: Who's that? (*We smile, long pause.*) Me?

Coach:	Only you. Without a compass and a sense of direction your boat is simply lost at sea.
Simon:	Mmm (*pause*). I never ask myself for direction
Coach:	Yes I know. How do you feel in your search?
Simon:	Lost.
Coach:	How might you set sail differently?
Simon:	(*Pause*) By deciding up front what I need, maybe.
Coach:	Excellent! How might you do that?

We explored how, rather than asking others continually for direction, Simon could set his own by being much more conscious of what he wanted, and naming this intention from the start in meetings and to the people with whom he interacted.

One month later, in our next coaching session:

Simon:	I had a revelation last time – and it has changed me.
Coach:	Tell me more?
Simon:	Intention – setting my intention has changed me.
Coach:	How?
Simon:	I feel more in control, my confidence is building and I am trusting in my own judgement much more than before.
Coach:	What is the difference you experience?
Simon:	I'm not as needy and people are surprised when I state my intention. I hadn't realised how I was constantly trying to work out what others wanted and meeting their expectations, forgetting about myself. I have a greater self-worth now. I listen to me more.

Coach:	When we met the first time, on a scale of 1 to 10, how were you feeling in terms of self-worth and confidence?
Simon:	A 3 or 4.
Coach:	What about now, after what you have learned around your intention and how you are using this?
Simon:	It's a 7.
Coach:	Taking charge and consciously setting your course has served you well – your confidence and self-worth have shifted. What might make it an 8 or 9?
Simon:	Practice (*we smile*).

Observe the difference that one coaching session can sometimes make to the client's self-esteem and worth. Part of the work of the coach is to remind the client and help them to utilise their inner resourcefulness, including the power of intention. This is an important faculty of mastery.

INTUITION

The second faculty that we more consciously discover together with the masterful coach is intuition. This is when, through our expanded awareness, we suddenly catch a glimpse of the larger field in which we are a part. It seems to be a direct vision and experience of reality simply as it is. Maybe we see wholeness before it is reasoned and rationalised.

The masterful coach is often highly intuitive and conscious of the importance of these sudden glimpses, aware of how they can inform the receptive mind and heart, and offer new important possibilities. Being sensitive and willing to respond to intuition is

n essential aspect of the masterful coach. It can give clues and
often a deeper insight into what is important to the client.

PAUSE POINT

**How do you employ intuition in your coaching practice?
What is its specific value to your work?**

I recently worked with a human resources director, Veronica. In
our first session, I intuitively saw her quite transfigured
through my mind's eye. This may seem very strange, but intuition can be. The question is if and how we can work with it.
The following extract is taken from our first session.

Veronica: I have a large business responsibility and too
              much work.

*From out of nowhere I suddenly saw my client in my mind's eye
wearing a white wedding dress and veil. I immediately connected
this with a princess from a fairytale in a Walt Disney production.
This happened two or three times while my client was speaking,
although Veronica was wearing a formal business suit. I inwardly
smiled, recognising my intuition and its strangeness, and, by trusting
it, I decided to explore.*

Coach: What are your favourite pastimes?
Veronica: I don't have a pastime with the children.
Coach: Mmm (*pause*). What about your favourite
              DVD?

*A favourite DVD, film or book can often give insight to the deep
aspirations of your client and what they particularly value and care
about.*

Veronica:	I'm a bit shy to share that.
Coach:	Why Veronica?
Veronica:	It's a children's DVD.
Coach:	I'm curious now.
Veronica:	It's called *The Princess Bride*.

I was quite astonished that this fitted so well with the wedding dress I'd visualised before with my intuitive eye.

Coach:	Why is the DVD so important to you?
Veronica:	It's full of hope and has a happy ending.

Although I remain deeply curious of the importance of the DVD and the central character to Veronica, we never fully completed the work. Veronica found herself facing a major work change and quite a traumatic period and decided, for whatever reason, to step out of the coaching relationship. Veronica may return to continue with the coaching at some point, but until then I am left very curious about the deeper significance and importance of *The Princess Bride*.

The masterful coach is able to completely trust and value the client's intuition as well as their own. The reaction of the analytical eye is to dismiss these irrational thoughts. One of the gifts of the masterful coach is to be able to include what may seem totally irrational as a way to provide an important new context for learning and development. This is demonstrated in the following case study.

I was working with a senior finance director, Sam, a prominent and responsible figure in his organisation. We were exploring the model of the three eyes. We had examined the analytical and appreciative eyes, and were now moving to explore the creative eye.

Sam has a strong rational side, and the vision of the analytical eye can at times dominate his outlook and approach to work and life. Increasingly, he has found that when he created space at weekends he was unable to relax properly. The demanding 'shoulds and musts' of the analytical eye were invading his need for down-time. In the following coaching conversation we arrive at an exploration of the creative eye.

Coach: One way I think of the creative eye is with this (*I place a coin out of my pocket on the table in front of Sam and smile*).

Sam: How does this relate to the creative eye?

Coach: The creative eye opens when you consider the analytical and appreciative eyes to be like two sides of the same coin. Their limitations balance out and a new way of seeing is now possible.

Sam: It reminds me of university.

Coach: Tell me more.

Sam: I loved 'systems thinking' at university. My tutor used to call finance a safe study. I was very interested in systems thinking and wanted to explore that much more.

Has my client had an intuition – as systems thinking has just entered his mind seemingly from nowhere? I start to muse about what might be happening and the importance and relevance of this intuition to Sam. Why now?

Coach: What did your reading on systems thinking give you?

Sam: It was different, exciting. I wanted to study it.

Coach: I wonder if your chance to read more on this topic is being presented once more?

Sam:	How come?
Coach:	The creative eye differs from both the analytical and appreciative eyes in that its vision can accommodate a third dimension – the universal. We can expand our vision to appreciate the larger system in which we live and work through the creative eye.
Sam:	Is that so?
Coach:	Trust your intuition, it's not by chance that you have connected with systems thinking – you may be being invited to do so once more.
Sam:	How interesting.

IMAGINATION

The writer Thomas Moore kindly composed the preface to my last book and, while doing so, emphasised the central importance of the imagination by reminding us of *oculus imaginationis* – the all-seeing eye of the imagination. This eye literally gives form to our sense and shapes our thoughts and experiences into new possibility. Through the imagination we encounter the world. Our minds travel to explore imaginatively what might or will be.

Through the imagination we can re-energise, open up and experience something more of the present, past or future. Your past can be re-imagined in the present. Through the active imagination of the creative eye we can feel our way into different situations and places.

The imagination enters the virtual, wanting to make it real

Imagination is the great sculpture and artist and is enlivened and increasingly active through the discovery of the masterful coach. When clients feel stuck they can conjure up an image or metaphor of where they might like to be. That representation of their experience of being stuck can also be a bridge to change. The imagination is our natural bridge between form and experience and is a vital part of coaching practice. Let me share with you an example from recent coaching work.

PAUSE POINT

How do you use imagination in your coaching practice? What is its specific value to your work?

Ruby is a senior leader within a major international organisation. She has recently been frustrated and angry, and has behaved badly in senior board meetings. She wishes to explore what's going on in more detail.

Ruby: I get angry, frustrated and then start to become quite disruptive.

Coach: What does that look like?

Ruby: I behave badly in the room.

Coach: Have you discovered a saboteur, I wonder?

Ruby: Yes, but I didn't realise just how disruptive I may have been.

Coach: Would you like to get to know this character a little more?

Ruby: Yes.

Coach: Imagine him or her to be a character of some sort, standing here with us now. What sort of character would he or she be – what size, shape, features, colour?

194 • THE COACHING SECRET

I invite Ruby to employ her active imagination in order to meet with this character more fully.

Ruby:	He's dark, very dark. Large, very sharp, incisive and masculine.
Coach:	Anything more?
Ruby:	I think he wears a mask.
Coach:	Do you have a name for him?
Ruby:	(*Laughs*) Let's call him (*pause*) Darth Vader.
Coach:	I can certainly see his power to disrupt now (*we laugh*). How does he limit your work?
Ruby:	(*Pause*) He causes problems, he tries to disrupt and spoil things.
Coach:	So he seems to limit you by being highly disruptive in important meetings. How does he serve you?
Ruby:	(*Pause*) I don't know.
Coach:	Stay with it Ruby.
Ruby:	(*Pause*) He stands up for the part of me that doesn't get seen.
Coach:	Say more?
Ruby:	(*Pause*) I've just realised that he comes out when I feel overlooked and not included. I have a lot to say, but I somehow can't get in to say it, or don't feel invited in. I get so angry because of this, and so I send in Darth.
Coach:	So Darth comes out when you feel excluded and can't add your significant experience to the discussions?
Ruby:	Yes.

Coach:	So you want to contribute and show your value and if that doesn't happen you send in Darth to create a little havoc?
Ruby:	Mmm (*pause*). That's true – exactly so.
Coach:	I know Darth is serving you, but how is he affecting your reputation, Ruby?
Ruby:	Wow, well (*pause*), he's not doing me any favours. I get so angry.
Coach:	If your anger had a voice, what would it say?
Ruby:	(*Long pause*) I am invisible and I have so much to say. It probably says, help me out! So I can share my experience.
Coach:	I imagine that's very frustrating for you.

Here I am empathising – I can see how hard this experience is for Ruby and how it is troubling her.

Ruby:	It is.
Coach:	What are you learning from this – in giving Darth shape and form?
Ruby:	He's a bit of an overkill and it's doing my reputation no good.
Coach:	Could you contract with Darth?
Ruby:	How?
Coach:	Can he help you to come in, in some way, rather than trashing the place (*smile*)?
Ruby:	Maybe (*pause*). When Darth comes out and I'm angry, he can maybe remind me that I need to speak out and bring my experience in. Maybe he can stand and guard me while I try?
Coach:	Would his presence help you in this way?
Ruby:	Yes, I might not feel so alone.

Coach:	So you can contract with him to be a protector and an aid rather than be totally disruptive (*smile*)?
Ruby:	Yes, I can.
Coach:	May the force be with you (*we laugh*).

Note how my client is able to give form, shape and character through her imagination to an aspect of her personality, Darth. Ruby then explores how she might more consciously direct the behaviour of Darth to help her.

As work with Ruby continued, she surprised her senior colleagues by not being disruptive, but asking their help to make sure that she could bring her experience and knowledge into the group. This allowed her to make a significant and important contribution at board level and feel much more satisfied in her work. I still hold a treasured picture of Ruby and Darth sitting together at the board meeting.

INTEGRITY

As you develop your coaching practice, your integrity will deepen. In this way I consider it to be an emerging faculty that we consciously discover together with the masterful coach.

Integrity is the satisfaction that comes from feeling more whole, complete and accepting of our truest nature

Let us briefly revisit and summarise how integrity is deepened through the coaching relationship. We judge and divide the self, rejecting what we label as bad. These banished aspects are pushed away, ultimately beyond our conscious awareness. We create a safe but divided and partial self that longs to be more whole and complete. The client turns to the coach to understand more fully and illuminate their hidden desires and the wish to change and develop. Through this trusting relationship – by examining behaviours, needs and aspirations – these denied and hidden aspects can once more be made conscious and be accepted back.

What was hidden or unconscious can be discerned by the shared vision of the coaching relationship and given back to the care of the client.

At the heart of coaching is a process of discovery, acceptance and reintegration

Through acceptance and deepening self-awareness, the client aspires to become more honest to their true nature and to experience wholeness – their original self. This aspiration deepens the authenticity and integrity in ourselves and how we relate. Returning for a moment to the jigsaw analogy, coaching helps the client not only to identify the pieces, but also, if each piece is accepted, how they fit together to become an *integrated* whole.

• PRESENCE AND PRESENCING •

The faculties of intuition, imagination, intention and integrity offer a remarkable sensitivity to orientate, discern, relate and resolve. Collectively they inform the 'presence' of the coach. What we mean by the experience of presence is not easy to describe.

Presence has a number of different dimensions. It describes the qualities of mastery in the coaching relationship – for example, your experience of a highly responsive, calm and deeply attentive coach. Presence, or 'presencing', may also describe an activity – the coach can help the client to feel the presence of the larger energetic field in which they participate. The coach who has discovered mastery can help to conceive and inform the larger context – the universal field – in which the client participates. The ideal future and the person we most aspire to be are both awaiting our attention and conscious expression. Might these already exist in potential and prospect?

Another way of thinking about the inner process of presencing is that we are drawn through our longing to make conscious the presence of our original being. Presence and being are intimately related.

> ## Presence maybe reflects our capacity to express the original self from which the qualities of mastery originate

To conclude this chapter, let us now explore some of the qualities of mastery that inform presence.

• THE QUALITIES OF MASTERY •

Many years ago, as a biochemist, I researched the impact of pesticides on aquatic life. It often involved going out on the Scottish lochs to sample the fish life. My colleagues, guiding the small boat, would remind me that when the weather is bad (as was commonly the case!) the fish go deeper and are much harder to catch. This made fishing much more challenging. Similar to the fish, when our own surface waters are choppy and chaotic, or when we are distracted, our qualities seem to go deeper within and remain hidden. It is only when we discover a period of calm that our deeper qualities, like the fish, can re-emerge, surface and find expression.

The more we learn how to still ourselves through the discovery of the inner compass, the more we can experience the presence and power of our inner qualities in practice. Such qualities may include compassion, peace and wisdom.

With the opening of the appreciative eye, we discover empathy and our capacity to relate. With the emergence of the inner compass, our capacity to be still and attentive deepens. This stillness permits the qualities of compassion, peacefulness and wisdom to emerge into our practice. One very pertinent and enigmatic question to ask is: 'Is the difference we make through coaching more a consequence of how we are than what we do?' I recall one rather complex incident in my coaching practice where compassion played a vital role.

Edward is a very senior and visible leader, working at the highest levels of the organisation. We have a strong coaching relationship. One day I received a very distressed phone call from him. In a moment of being placed on the spot facing a large audience, he had spontaneously said something that was deemed by some of the audience to be inappropriate and offensive. Edward was distressed by his mistake and I agreed to meet with him immediately. Never have I seen someone so upset as a result of a mistake. He told me that he stood on the brink of resignation because of his error and the pressure from some key people.

We worked through what had happened and how he had apologised openly and specifically to those concerned and most impacted. I reassured Edward that I would support him through this period and we explored the next steps. I took my own experience of this session to supervision. I was deeply moved by the impact of this error on Edward and, with the guidance of my own experienced supervisor, I found myself asking 'Where in the organisation is the voice of compassion rather than judgement?'

This was a delicate and complex situation and not an easy one for any coach. I knew Edward's sponsor well through our coaching triangle – sponsor, client and coach. I contacted Edward and checked if he was OK with my speaking to his sponsor. He was. In that meeting I reflected with Edward's sponsor the dilemma that Edward faced. Edward had completely accepted his error and misjudgement and had apologised openly. Should this end the very successful career of someone who had made a major contribution to the success of the business and organisation and was quite exemplary to this point? I turned to his sponsor and asked: 'Where is the voice of compassion within this organisation?'

The sponsor was pensive and receptive and subsequently intervened at the highest levels to ask the same question of some of the key individuals involved. The result was that Edward did not resign and was allowed to stay and to work with his error. He owned his fallibility and grew through this experience. His successful career continues.

The boundaries of the coaching frame between the client and sponsor are not always clear. Ultimately, we may need to remind ourselves of our priorities and why we coach. Compassion is a key quality I strive to express in my work. It is a quality that reminds us of the importance of the conscience of the coach. With compassion, as in this case, we can discover and are humbled by our fallibility, and in accepting fallibility we give ourselves permission to be real and authentic. In becoming real and authentic, we discover the joy and freedom of mastery.

C h a p t e r   N i n e

SEEDS OF LEARNING

•••

Look back with me over the journey of writing this book, and indeed a career of coaching, and take with you a few seeds of learning that have fostered my growth and practice.

•••

• ESSENTIAL LEARNING •

PERMIT FALLIBILITY

Maybe the greatest gift we discover together with the masterful coach is an acceptance of our fallibility.

When we are fallible, we free our clients to explore their own fallibility

We free our humanity to find expression through our work. When we are free to be imperfect we can more fully relax into being our most natural self. Strangely, in acknowledging our limitations, we can often glimpse that which is unlimited. As we accept our limitations, paradoxically our confidence to coach increases, as we are no longer concerned with making mistakes. We may even realise how our problems and mistakes become a vital source of potential learning and growth.

YOU HOLD THE MASTER KEY

The key to mastery is in your hands. Commonly we meet other people's expectations and forget our own.

> Your unique individuality can easily be forgotten in seeking the approval of others

It often seems that our chance to feel good and fulfilled is dependent on meeting someone else's expectations and goals. In a topsy-turvy world the antithesis is nearer the truth. Fulfilment is something only you can discover and permit. In my own experience this comes from the continuing journey of self-acceptance, and is the joy of acknowledging your innate talents and what you most love and enjoy. Only you can permit yourself the joy, freedom and confidence of being your most natural self and there meet with the masterful coach.

IT DOESN'T HAVE TO BE HARD

We make things hard because we (our analytical eye) love the challenge. We set the bar we then need to jump. Maybe we believe somewhere deep down that work has to be hard in order to be worthwhile. Instead, find the choice to also make it easy. In striving and driving we lose sight of our natural talent and mastery. See if you can make it easy. Do more of what you most enjoy and love, without reproach.

> ## Give yourself permission to enjoy your life to the fullest – no one else can

BE AND DO

We can spend our lives searching for our most significant other – the person we most long to find and with whom we belong. But in the activity of the search and need to find we forget and overlook the being that exists within our doing. Our namesake reminds us that there is a human being within all that we do. Might this being be our most significant other? In discovering this being, do we make the acquaintance of the masterful coach as our most authentic identity as a human being?

BE COMFORTABLE WITH PARADOX

If you learn to see the paradox of things you no longer need to judge or divide. Instead, you are given the chance to contemplate more deeply dilemma and conflict and to consider if there might be a deeper, more peaceful resolution. Paradox can teach us how to see the prospect of a more creative resolution beneath surface conflict, division and difference.

> ## Paradox teaches the judge within us the wisdom of patience

BE STILL

We often fill our lives with activity. The qualities that define and inform our mastery emerge when we are still. Our goal is not so much to get somewhere, but is more the chance to come home to our truest and most natural self. The masterful coach awaits your acquaintance just beyond your busyness. When we are still we can see the extent of our activity, rather than be driven by it. We can give our full attention and concentration to the coaching relationship and practice.

Learn how to still your surface waters in order to discover your depth

REMEMBER THAT WE FORGET
If you remember anything – remember that we forget. Forgetting is a fallibility that we learn to forgive. In the humility of forgiving yourself and others you recognise the strength of the masterful coach.

YOUR LOCK IS THE KEY
We label problems as bad and rationalise or reject them.

In dividing ourselves we split and trap our potential

The partial self seeks always to become whole. In becoming whole we realise our hidden potential as the power to choose, relate, resolve, develop, learn and change. Maybe our ultimate power as human beings is realised in the expression of original self? The journey of the coach is to accept partiality and to foster unity. The problem we consider to be our lock in truth is the key to our hidden potential and power. Rather than seeing problems as a limitation, let these serve as the base from which we remember our potentiality and aspiration to wholeness.

EVERYTHING SERVES AND LIMITS
We confine ourselves when we divide and judge – we split our resources and our resourcefulness. When you face a problem as

a coach, consider how it both serves and limits and therein you will discover the hidden potential. Try it.

COACH WITH YOUR HEART AS WELL AS YOUR HEAD

How you are when you coach is as important as what you do. If the client can trust and know how much you truly care, then nothing more is usually necessary. Knowing we are valued in our imperfect state, and knowing this is natural, can offer the greatest freedom and joy. If you build trust, care and compassion then you permit your client to be their most natural self without condition – and all this may happen without words.

PLANT SEEDS

I never forget the joy of gardening. Ultimately, growth is out of my hands and yet I can nurture, care and dream of creating my own small Eden. Watching how nature grows is a great teacher for the coach. All we can do is plant our seeds timely, thought-fully, compassionately, and playfully – with the intention and hope that they will grow, blossom and fruit. This is the essence of my own coaching practice.

PAUSE POINT

What seeds of learning are most relevant to your practice? Do you have additional essential learning from your own practice?

Chapter Ten

CONCLUSION

• • •

Mastery is the capacity to focus purely on the activity of coaching. We think it is something we can be taught, but it is not. It is something we learn through our own experience from the inside out. The secret to becoming an exceptional coach is to realise that mastery is not a destiny we can strive to reach. To be masterful necessitates that we discover the masterful being within. It is this being that informs your mastery.

When we meet this inner coach, our vision expands, our capacity and quality of how we relate deepens, and our ability to resolve conflict emerges. We refine ourselves from the inside out; no one else can do it for us. We learn that mastery is the art of minimising our inner distractions so that we can place our attentiveness and concentration purely on the activity of coaching itself.

The identity of the masterful coach is our most authentic being. Every coach is an apprentice to the self – we are ultimately self-taught. Mastery is not only what we aspire to be or become, it is our origin, it is our most natural talent. The practice of coaching offers the chance for us to discover this inner teacher and master our practice. I often think that coaching is more a self-fulfilling prophecy than a profession. As I discover and accept myself, so I am inspired to discover more.

Commonly, coaching is a means to improve performance. It is, however, in essence an act intent on discovering the source of our deepest acts of humanity. It affirms our innate talent together with a masterful being. This new found depth deepens the quality of how we relate enabling sustained change through building relationships and community.

Discovering the masterful coach necessitates that we let go of who we think we are. It is remarkable to me, in a world busily seeking approval and qualification, that mastery is found in our courage to let go of what we know. In willingly entering into the mystery of our unknown, we are propelled towards mastery.

If you have found the instruments that can help you to navigate and set your own course in this unknown – from the inside out – then the seas, be they calm or stormy, are but a rite of passage. Relax, be yourself, give yourself permission to be who you are without condition or reproach. Live the things you love – be happy in your work. It doesn't have to be hard. This is the legacy of the masterful coach. Through the practice of coaching we discover our deeper authenticity – the self we were born to be. If we are this without condition then we fulfil a larger destiny by returning to our origin.

SUGGESTED READING

...

The following books offer contrasting perspectives on coaching and the scope of the field:

Gallwey, W.T. (2001) *The Inner Game of Work – Focus, Learning, Pleasure and Mobility in the Workplace.* Random House of Canada Limited, Toronto.

Downey, M. (2003) *Effective Coaching: Lessons from the Coach's Coach.* Texere, New York.

Orem, S.L., Binkert, J. and Clancy, A.L. (2007) *Appreciative Coaching: A Positive Process for Change.* Josey-Bass, San Franciso.

The following books offer a dynamic model of self and how we emerge and grow:

Assagioli, R. (1975) *Psychosynthesis: A Manual of Principles and Techniques.* Turnstone Books, London.

Ferrucci, P. (1990) *Inevitable Grace: Breakthroughs in the Lives of Great Men and Women: Guides to Your Self-Realization.* Jeremy P. Tarcher Inc., Los Angeles.

Moore, T. (2001) *Original Self – Living with Parallax and Originality.* Published by Perennial, an imprint of HarperCollins Publishers, New York.

The following provides insight into the nature and experience of flow:

Csikszentmihalyi, M. (2002) *Flow: The Classic Work on How to Achieve Happiness*. Harper Row, New York.

Finally, this text offers insights into presence and presencing:

Senge, P., Scharmer, C.O., Jaworsky, J. and Flowers, B.S. (2005) *Presence: Exploring Profound Change in People, Organizations and Society*. Nicholas Brealey, London.

INDEX

• • •